Linux

This book includes

Linux for Beginners + Kali Linux Hacking

The Comprehensive Step-by-Step Guide to Learn the Fundamentals of Cyber Security, Penetration Testing, Networking and Computer Hacking. Include Exercises and Self-Evaluation Tests.

By: Ethem Mining

Copyright © 2020 – All rights reserved.

No part of this publication may be reproduced, duplicated or transmitted in any form or by any means, electronic, mechanical, scanning, photocopying, recording or otherwise without prior written permission from the publisher. All rights reserved.

The information provided herein is stated to be truthful and consistent in that any liability, regarding inattention or otherwise, by any usage or abuse of any policies, processes or directions contained within is the solitary and complete responsibility of the recipient reader. Under no circumstances will any legal liability or blame be held against the publisher for any reparation, damages or monetary loss due to the information herein, either directly or indirectly.

Legal Notice.

This book is copyright protected. This is only for personal use. You cannot amend, distribute, sell, quote, use or paraphrase any part of the content within this book without the consent of the author or copyright owner. Legal action will be pursued if this is breached.

Disclaimer Notice.

Please note the information contained within this document is for educational and entertainment purposes only. This book not intended to be a substitute for medical advice. Please consult your health care provider for medical advice and treatment.

Table of Contents

Introduction 11
Chapter 1: What is Linux? 13
    What is an Operating System? 13
    Linux as an Operating System 18
    From Unix to Linux 21
    Systems Architecture of Linux 22
    File Hierarchy Structure of Linux 24
    The Process Architecture of Linux 27
Chapter 1 Answer Key 32
Chapter 2: Choose Your Distribution 33
    What is a Linux Distribution? 34
    How to Choose the Right Distribution for You 35
    Ubuntu 36
    Linux Mint 37
    MX Linux 38
    openSUSE 39
    Fedora 40
    Debian GNU/Linux 41
    Arch Linux 42
    Slackware 43
    Gentoo 44
    CentOS 45
Chapter 2 Quiz 47
Chapter 2 Answer Key 48
Chapter 3: Install Linux 49
    What is a Virtual Machine? 49
    Installing Linux on Physical Hardware 52
    Installing Linux on Virtual Machines on Windows 10 55
    Installing Linux on Virtual Machines on macOS High Sierra 57
Chapter 3 Quiz 59
Chapter 3 Answer Key 60
Chapter 4: Linux Shell 61
    What is Shell? 62
    Gaining Access to the Shell 63
    Types of Shell 67
    Shell Scripting 69
    Basic Command Line Editing 72
Chapter 4 Quiz 73
Chapter 4 Answer Key 74

Chapter 5: Linux Commands 75

    System Information Commands 76
    System Shutdown, Restart, and Logout Commands 78
    Files and Directory Commands 81
    Users and Groups Commands 85
    Files Permissions Commands 87
    Archives and Compressed Files Commands 88

Chapter 5 Quiz 89

Chapter 5 Answer Key 90

Chapter 6: Control Privileged User 91

    Types of Linux Accounts 91
    Sudo 95
    The Sudoers File 98

Chapter 6 Quiz 101

Chapter 6 Answer Key 102

Chapter 7: Basic Network Administration 103

    Networking 101 103
    The Network Extension 104
    The Network Topology 106
    Main Protocols of the Internet 107
    Diagnostic commands 112

Chapter 7 Quiz 113

Chapter 7 Answer Key 114

Chapter 8: Alternatives to Windows Applications 115

    Microsoft Office Substitute 116
    MS Notepad Substitute 117
    Internet Explorer Substitute 118
    Photoshop Substitute 118
    Movie Maker Substitute 119
    Windows Media Center Substitute 120
    Adobe Acrobat Reader Substitute 120

Chapter 8 Quiz 123

Chapter 8 Answer Key 124

Conclusion 125

Introduction 131

Part I 133

Introduction to Kali Linux and Hacking 133

Chapter 9: Introduction to Hacking 135

What is Hacking?..136
Malware...137
Session Hijacking...138
SQL Injection...138
Phishing...139
DOS...139
Reasons for Hacking...141
Black Hats...142
Grey Hats..142
Red Hats..143
Green Hats...143
Blue Hats...143
Script Kiddies..144
Hacktivists..144
White Hat (Ethical Hacking)..144
What is Cybersecurity?...146
The Elements of Cybersecurity..147
Information Security: The CIA Triad..148
Confidentiality...149
Integrity..149
Availability..150

Chapter 10: Introduction to Networking 151

What is a Network?..151
Types of Networks..152
    LAN...153
    WAN..153
    VPN..153
Network Address...154
Nodes...154
Hosts..155
IP Address..155
Public vs. Private IP address...156
Assigning an IP address...156
Protocol Layers..159
    Internet Protocol (IP)...159
    The TCP/IP Model...160
Threats to Network Security..162
    Man-in-the-Middle..163
    Cyberattacks...164
    DOS and DDOS..165
    MAC Spoofing..165

Chapter 11: Kali Linux: The Hacker Operating System 167

What is Linux?..167
What is Kali Linux?..169
Should I use Kali Linux?...171
Kali Linux Features..173

Hundreds of Penetration Testing Tools 173
Free 173
Secure 173
Customizable 173
Multi-Language Support 174
Open Source Git Tree 174
FHS Compliant 174
Wireless Device Support 174
Custom Kernel 174
How to Install Kali Linux 175
What You Need for Installation 175
Creating the Bootable USB with Linux 179

Chapter 12: Basic Linux Commands 181

The Terminal 181
Command Prompts 182
Executing the Commands 182
Archives 184
Directory Navigation 185
Disk Usage 185
File and Directory Commands 186
File Transfers 187
Hardware Information Commands 187
Installing Packages 188
Networking 189
Performance Monitoring 190
Process Management 191
Search 192
SSH Logins 193
System Information Commands 193
User Information and Management Commands 194

Part II 197

Kali Linux Hacking 197

Chapter 13: Nmap and Detecting and Exploiting Vulnerabilities 199

What is Nmap? 199
How to Use Nmap to Understand and Exploit Vulnerabilities 200
Scanning Commands 201
Scanning Techniques and Commands 202
TCP SYN Scan 203
TCP Connect() Scan 203
UDP Scan 203
FIN Scan 204
Ping Scan 204
Version Detection 205
Idle Scanning 205
Penetration Testing 205

  Pre-Engagement 206
  Reconnaissance 207
 Threat Modeling and Identifying Vulnerabilities 207
  Exploitation 209
  Post-Exploitation 209
  Reporting 210
  Retesting 210
Chapter 14: How to Become and Remain Anonymous **211**
 Proxychains 212
 VPN 214
 Tor and Kali Linux 217
Chapter 15: Metasploit Framework **221**
 What is Metasploit? 221
 Metasploit Users 222
 Metasploit Modules 223
 Using Metasploit 224
 Installing Metasploit 225
 Managing the Metasploit Database 225
 The Metasploit Datastore 226
 The Metasploit Workspaces 227
Chapter 16: Digital Certificate **229**
 What is a Digital Certificate? 230
 Certificate Authorities 231
 Types of Certificates 231
  Root Certificate 232
  Intermediate Certificate 232
  SSL Certificate 233
 Generating Self-Signed SSL Certificates 233
Chapter 17: Bash and Python Scripting **235**
Conclusion **241**

Linux for Beginners

A Practical and Comprehensive Guide to Learn Linux Operating System and Master Linux Command Line. Contains Self-Evaluation Tests to Verify Your Learning Level

By: Ethem Mining

Introduction

If you have picked up this book, you are inevitably interested in Linux, at least to some degree. You may be interested in understanding the software, or debating whether it is right for you. However, especially as a beginner, it is easy to feel lost in a sea of information. How do you know what version of Linux to download? Or how to even go about downloading it, to begin with? Is Linux even right for you to begin with? All of those are valid questions, and luckily for you, *Linux for Beginners* is here to guide you through all of it.

Linux is an operating system, much like iOS and Windows. It can be used on laptops, large computer centers, on cell phones, and even smart fridges. If it can be programmed, Linux can almost definitely be installed, thanks to several features and benefits. Linux is small, secure, supported on other devices, and incredibly easy to customize. With Linux, you can create a setup that is exactly what you want, with privacy, security, and access to plenty of free to use software.

This means that, once you develop the knowhow, you can create a customized experience that will do exactly what you need, allowing yourself to optimize the setup you have and ensure that the setup you have

As you read through this book, you will be given a comprehensive guide to everything you need to know as a beginner to Linux. You will learn about why and how to determine which distribution of Linux is right for you. You will discover how to use the terminal, how to set up exactly what you will need on your system, and more. When you are able to make your customized setup however you see fit, this means that you can make sure that you are always working within the constraints of the hardware that you are using.

This means that older machines, which may struggle under a load of many modern operating systems such as Windows 10, can be optimized and used to their fullest potential without wasting valuable resources or processing power on aspects that are unnecessary, redundant, or even just detrimental to whatever it is that you need to do.

Ultimately, you will be provided with exactly what you need to know to get started with Linux, from start to finish. You will even be provided with several alternatives to Windows-specific applications that can be downloaded and used while running Linux on your device. Everything will be provided in the simplest terms possible, so you get a complete and thorough understanding of exactly what you need to know if you wish to get started with Linux, and at the end of each chapter, you will be given a short, five question quiz, as well as the answers to ensure that you are, in fact, comprehending the material that has been provided. Between receiving several step-by-step guides, questions, and lists of commands, you should have much of what you need to know to at least get started with the installation of your own distribution of Linux!

There are plenty of books on this subject on the market, thanks again for choosing this one! Every effort was made to ensure it is full of as much useful information as possible; please enjoy!

Chapter 1: What is Linux?

So, you have decided that you want to use Linux—or at least learn more about it than you already know. You are in the right place! Within this chapter, you will develop an understanding of what Linux is. First, you will discuss what operating systems are to develop the foundational information you will need to guide you through the rest of the book. From there, you will discuss Linux as an operating system, learning what it has to offer and why it is so commonly used by other people. From there, you will learn how Linux came to be. Lastly, you will begin to learn how Linux is composed, looking at the systems architecture, file hierarchy, and processes.

What is an Operating System?

An operating system, commonly abbreviated as OS, is the program that runs the hardware of a computer. In running the hardware, it also allows for the management and usage of the software. It also allows for the interaction between the user and the hardware, facilitating acts such as input and output.

It is essentially the intermediary, allowing the hardware to run the programs and the programs to make use of the hardware.

Of course, this means that the operating system is the single most important piece of software that you will ever run—without it, your computer will not be able to manage the hardware. Think of the OS as the brain of the computer. Just as your brain keeps your body running properly and reacts to interaction, so too does the OS keep the computer running properly and allow it to interact with the computer. When you use an operating system, you are essentially interacting with a program that allows you to speak to the computer, commanding it to do whatever you expect it to do without having to speak in a way that the computer understands. It is the translator, the intermediary, that allows you and the computer to interact, and without it, the computer is entirely useless.

The operating system's important job

As briefly touched upon, the operating system's job is to manage all software and hardware on the computer. Software refers to the programming on a computer—it is a list of instructions on how a computer should handle and process certain information in order to properly perform the tasks that you have commanded. It ranges from programs, such as running your internet browser or playing a video file all the way to the system running your computer. Each of these programs is what you have your computer to do, and the operating system makes sure it is run properly while also utilizing the hardware.

Hardware is the physical computer itself and all of the components that make it up. This includes the motherboard, the central processing unit (CPU), RAM, graphics processing unit (GPU), hard drive, power supply, and all other components that you use, such as the monitor, mouse, and keyboard, and anything else hooked up to your computer to use it. Each of these computer components has their own specific purposes, which come together to allow for the processing of the computer software installed.

Hardware

- The physical components of the computer, such as GPU, CPU, RAM, and all peripheral devices

Software

- The programs containing instructions that tell the computer to handle any input and data that arrives

Operating System

- Manages and facilitates the function of both the hardware and software together with the commands of the user.

The operating system helps juggle all of those components together while also simultaneously managing the software and any user input, allowing for the computer to run. It ensures that each program that is functioning is able to access the proper hardware support necessary without infringing on the function of other programs at the same time. Essentially, the operating system manages it all to give you the smooth and seamless functioning you have come to expect from your technology through the following functions:

- **Command interpretation:** Allows for the translation of the commands given to the computer
- **Communication management:** Allows for the coordination and assigning of software resources
- **Device management:** Manages the usage of all devices

- **File management:** Manages any processes and activities related to files, such as organization, naming, retrieving, sharing, or securing

- **Input/Output management:** Translates and manages inputs and outputs

- **Job accounting:** Tracks the time needed and necessary resources by jobs and users

- **Memory management:** Allows for the allocation and de-allocation of memory that programs are in need of at any given moment

- **Networking:** Allows for processors that are not sharing any memory or hardware to communicate resources or data

- **Processor management:** Helps the operating system create and delete processes, facilitates synchronization, and allows for communication between processes that may be interacting with each other

- **Secondary storage management:** Makes sure that data is stored in the right storage to be accessed when needed

- **Security:** Protects the data stored within a computer system from any malware or unauthorized attempts to access it

Types of operating system

Given the wide range of functions for the operating system, it should come as no surprise that there are several different types of OS that all serve different purposes and come with their own strengths and weaknesses. This section will provide a brief overview of the varying types of OS as well as the most common usage scenarios for them.

- **Batch operating system:** Designed to run jobs with similar needs that have been grouped together. The user is never directly interacting with the computer. Instead, the job is prepared offline and submitted to the computer operator to process. This is reserved for lengthy processes.

- **Multitasking/time-sharing operating systems:** This type of OS allows people at a different terminal (shell) to use the same computer at the same time. The CPU gets shared between the multiple users.

- **Real time OS:** These systems have minimal latency (lag between input/output) to allow for the response time to be nearly immediate. Ideal for military or space software systems that need to be able to react nearly instantly.

- **Network Operating System:** This OS runs on a server that is then accessible from several locations at once.

- **Distributed Operating System:** An extension of the network operating system, this type of OS makes use of several processors in several different machines, allowing for high-efficiency computing and processing.

- **Mobile OS:** This is any OS that is designed specifically for mobile devices, such as smartphones and tablets. The most commonly used mobile operating systems include Android and iOS.

Commonly used operating systems

Most of the time, any computer you buy will come with some sort of operating system already installed and ready to go. This means that if you want to use most products right out of the box, you can choose to do so. However, you can also upgrade them or change out your operating system for another one if you find that another one. For the most part, the choice of operating system is primarily a matter of preference, though some OS will come with different software compatibility.

Perhaps the starkest difference between operating systems will be the graphical user interface (GUI- pronounced as gooey). The GUI is what you see on your display when you are using your computer and allows you to interact with your software, and in turn, hardware. This will be the combination of graphics and text that you see on your screen. While the GUI may be different between OS, they will all bring with them the same basic features and functions.

Nevertheless, if you have a preference for one type of OS over the other, that is a valid matter of opinion, and the one you choose should be the OS that works best for you. Nevertheless, take a moment to familiarize yourself with the three most common operating systems you will encounter from day to day: Microsoft Windows, macOS, and Linux.

- **Microsoft Windows:** Created in the mid-1980s, this is the most popular OS you will encounter in varying versions. The most recent is Windows 10, which was released in 2015. Nearly any personal computer (PC) that you will buy comes preinstalled with Windows, with the most notable exception being Apple products. It is fairly versatile in what the user can do, and is constantly getting updates to keep it secure.

- **macOS:** Preloaded on Macintosh computers, macOS is much less popular. It is calculated that less than 10% of the global operating systems are utilizing macOS. It looks sleeker but is typically only works with proprietary software and peripherals. Altogether, between the three operating systems, macOS is going to be the most expensive to run to its fullest capabilities. Because of this, macOS is a bit more on the restrictive end in usage and customizability, with many common programs, games, and other software not being macOS compatible. However, the macOS tends to be on the less-hacked side, making it perhaps a bit more secure.

- **Linux:** Linux is a bit different than the other two—unlike the proprietary Windows and macOS, Linux is open-source. This means that it can be modified by anyone and distributed around the world for free. This makes Linux the least restrictive of the three major operating systems you will encounter, and yet it makes up less than 2% of the global operating systems in use. Despite this statistic, most servers will utilize Linux thanks to the versatility and customizability.

Linux as an Operating System

Linux, then, is an OS that is open-source—this means that it is readily customized and altered. Open-source operating systems are free to run, free to alter, and free to distribute, whether you have altered it or not.

This means, then, that there are many different distributions of Linux floating around out there, as each person who has ever made a change or customized version for themselves is free to redistribute their own version. However, these distributions will be discussed in depth in Chapter 2.

Linux can be installed on a wide range of hardware, allowing for the development of software and running of applications. This OS was developed in the C programming language, and today, C is still the primary language used. Initially designed to be similar to UNIX, which will be discussed in the next subchapter, Linux has evolved far beyond its initial scope. It is now used on phones to supercomputers and everything in between. When you use Linux as an OS, you are utilizing the Linux kernel to manage the hardware, and then building up from that kernel to develop the rest of the OS with software. The operating system that you think of when you hear Linux is actually an assortment of several different pieces. These pieces all work in tandem to allow the software programmed to function. These core pieces are the bootloader, the kernel, the init system, daemons, the graphical server, the desktop environment, and the applications that you install.

These pieces all serve various functions that will be crucial to your ability to actually run the OS in the first place.

- **Bootloader:** This is the software that will boot the computer—this means that it will make trigger the operating system to start running. Most of the time, there will be a quick splash screen that will display, letting you know that the OS is booting up. The splash screen will disappear as soon as the OS is ready to function, and that time is largely dependent upon the hardware that is running it. There are several different bootloaders, such as LILO (Linux Loader), LOADLIN (Load Linux), or GRUB (Grand Unified Bootloader).
- **Kernel:** This is where the actual name "Linux" came from. The Linux Kernel acts as the heart of the OS, allowing for the management of and interaction with the CPU, RAM, and all peripheral devices that are being used. It is the foundation for the rest of the OS, and without this kernel, you cannot run the device.
- **Init system:** This allows for the bootstrap, or activation, of the user space. Most often, you will see systemd as the init system.
- **Daemons:** These run several different background services that typically start on their own during the booting process or after you have logged onto the desktop. Think of daemons as background processes, and most often, you will see them in code with a "d" at the end, such as httpd as the web server daemon.

- **Graphical user interface (GUI):** This is a sub-system responsible for translating the computer data into the graphics displayed on your monitor of choice. A regularly used GUI in Linux is the X Window System, more commonly known as X.

- **Desktop environment:** This is the part of the graphics that you are actually able to interact with. There are several that are readily available depending on your own preference, with some of the more common ones being GNOME, Cinnamon, MATE, Unity, etc.

- **Applications:** These are just like applications on your phone. This is any sort of program or software downloaded to serve a specific purpose. There is nearly an endless supply of different applications that can be downloaded and utilized with Linux, including many that are readily available on the other operating systems as well, such as GIMP for image editing, Discord for chatting, Thunderbird for emails, and more. Chapter 8 will give you a rundown of several alternatives to common windows applications for more examples of common Linux apps available to you.

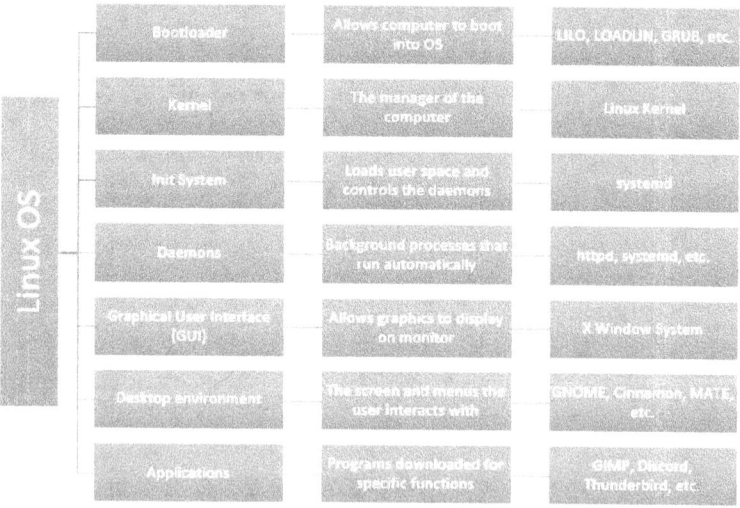

From Unix to Linux

What is now known as Linux began first with the development of Unix? Developed from the Multics project from the Bell Laboratories Computer Sciences Research Center, the goal was to create a multi-user OS that would have single-level storage, dynamic linking, and a hierarchical file system. However, this project was discontinued in 1969. Being discontinued did not deter a group of researchers, including Ken Thompson and Dennis Ritchie, to complete their project. Instead of Multics, however, they utilized the C programming language to rewrite their entire system, maintaining those core assets of Multics. In the end, they created Unix. The programming language made this OS unique—it was portable. This meant that it could be moved off of the hardware it was on, allowing data to live long past the hardware's life span.

This newly created Unix system was developed further and allowed to be adopted commercially. It eventually spread further within academia, with the creation of Berkeley Software Distribution (BSD). This was further developed into NeXTStep, which eventually grew to become the foundation for macOS, and MINIX, designed to be educational and eventually became the reference for Linux Torvalds to create Linux.

Unix and its successors primarily remained locked behind licensures, and many different developers began to work to create free alternatives. Among these were Richard Stallman, a researcher who worked for MIT at the time. He started work on what became known as GNU, which was distributed as open-source software beginning in 1985.

Torvalds, frustrated with the licensure for MINIX, began work on his own OS in 1991. It was reminiscent of MINIX, with beginning development done on MINIX with the use of the GNU C compiler. However, over time, it transformed into its own project with its own developers to separate it out, and in 1994, version 1.0 of the Linux kernel was released. This means that there were two major influences from Unix to Linux—GNU, which remains a prominent component of many different distributions of Linux, and the initial development of Linux done within the MINIX system.

Most commonly today, when you hear "Linux," you are most likely discussing the presence of both the Linux kernel and GNU. However, there are some systems, such as those on handheld devices, frequently use the Linux kernel with next to no GNU influence.

Systems Architecture of Linux

At this point, you have already seen a brief overview of the architecture of Linux—this is the breakdown of Linux that you saw in the chart earlier in the chapter. However, there are some details that need to be discussed in further depth. Within this section, you will learn more about the separation of user vs. kernel space, function of the Linux kernel, and the command line interface (CLI) known as a shell.

User space vs. kernel space

Wouldn't it be frustrating if you were working on your computer, having spent hours trying to solidify something that you were trying to accomplish, only to have the entire system shut down because it accidentally took up too much space for the OS to keep operating? Most people would agree that yes, it would be incredibly frustrating to have a program that would crash randomly due to running out of memory, and for that very reason, there is a special space dedicated solely to the OS on your memory in order to run it. Your OS will break your memory down into two categories, separating them out entirely and completely restricting them.

It creates a kernel space, which is designed to have enough space for the system to run in order to ensure that you never run out of space necessary to run the OS in the first place. It also creates an extra safeguard, protecting your OS from any tampering from outside sources that may have been downloaded or initiated within the user space. By creating that sort of divide, the kernel is protected, and your computer should function smoothly.

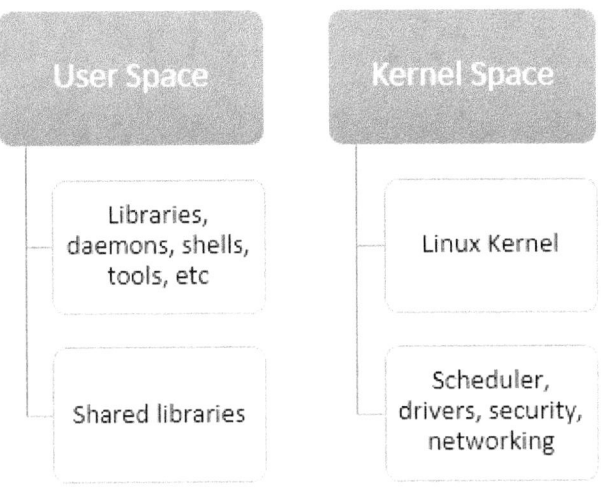

Every application must make system calls to the kernel within the kernel space if they wish to access system resources, such as making use of memory or network devices since the kernel is what tells the hardware to process in the first place.

The Linux Kernel

The Linux kernel is literally the namesake of the program itself and is crucial to understand. The kernel, as summed up earlier in the chapter, is the part of the operating system that controls the computer. The kernel acts as the mediator between the hardware and the operating system itself, allowing the OS to run applications in the first place. It schedules the order that applications will be run, accesses data, and even manages how memory is used within the computer. This is the initial part of the OS that is booted upon startup, and the kernel contains the most important parts of the OS code.

As depicted in this graphic above, you can see the relationship between the processes clearly—this is a more in-depth version of the graphic introduced in the beginning of the chapter, showing you the step between the OS and the hardware now that you have a better understanding of how the OS will work in the first place.

Command line interface (CLI)

Most often, Linux is administered from what is known as a command line interface (CLI). This is also commonly referred to as a shell. Chapter 4 will be dedicated to discussing shells in more depth, but you should have a general idea of what they are before continuing on. The shell is the program that allows you to input commands from a keyboard. Within Linux, the most commonly used program is bash (bourne again shell), which is an enhanced version of the original shell program used by Unix that was written by Steve Bourne.

However, you cannot access the shell without another program first that will enable you to communicate with the shell in the first place. This is known as your terminal emulator, and when you are able to install this, you are able to begin to interact with the terminal. Opening the terminal emulator will open up another window that will allow for the interaction via typed commands. Like the shells, these commands and instructions on how to start and use a terminal will come later in the book. At this point, it is enough for you to know that interacting with the OS directly is an option for you.

File Hierarchy Structure of Linux

In order to function as effectively as possible, Linux makes use of what is known as the Linux File Hierarchy Structure (FHS). This defines the directory structure and contents within Unix-like operating systems, such as Linux. This particular hierarchy is managed, maintain, and regulated thanks to the upkeep performed by the Linux Foundation.

When using the FHS, all files and directories can be found under the root directory /, even if they happen to be stored elsewhere physically or virtually. However, some directories exist only under certain circumstances, requiring a particular system with specific subsystems installed. Most directories that will be discussed in this section can be found in all Unix operating systems, and they are commonly utilized in the same way, though the descriptions you will receive in this subchapter should only be considered true for Linux.

/ (Root)
This is the primary root of the entire file system. Everything can be linked back to root. Only the root user will have permission to write or edit under /, and you will see /root as the root user's home directory. Note that /root is different from /.

/bin
This is a list of essential command binaries that must be available within single user mode. This will include binary executables, meaning files that are stored in binary format, making them readable to the computer, but not to humans. You will also find other common Linux commands for single-user modes within this directory.

/boot
These are your bootloader files. You will see files such as:

- **Kernel initrd:** initial RAM disk—allows for the initial ability for the boot loader to load a RAM disk.

- **Vmlinux:** ELF (executable and linkable format) based file that is the uncompressed version of the kernel image for debugging.

- **GRUB file:** The bootloader package.

/dev

These are essential device files. These may include terminal devices, devices attached to the system, or USB.

/etc
These files are host-specific but still system-wide configuration files. You will find all of your programs' various configuration files within this section, as well as the startup and shutdown shell scripts that will be necessary to either start or end your programs.

/home
This is where you will find personal settings, your files that you have saved, and home directories. If you have downloaded and saved it, it will be here. It will most likely save with your profile or computer name in a format like /home/NAMEHERE.

/lib
This is the home to any libraries that are necessary for the binary files that you have saved in /bin/ and /sbin/.

/media
This is where you will find mount points for removable media. Most often, you will see the name of the format of the mount here, such as /media/cdrom if you have insterted a CD, or /media/usb-drive for a USB drive.

/mnt
This refers to temporarily mounted files. In this directory, temporary filesystems can be mounted by sysadmins.

/opt
This refers to optional application software. These files will house add-on applications, and they should fall under /opt, or a subdirectory somewhere within /opt.

/proc
A virtual system that houses process and kernel information. Typically, this is automatically generated by the system, with information about the current running process.

/sbin
This is another file for binary executables, but /sbin files are typically used for maintenance purposes by the system admin.

/srv
Standing for "service," /srv holds data that is related to server-specific functions or services.

/tmp
These are temporary files that are most likely not going to be preserved when the system eventually shuts down and reboots. Typically, these are also restricted in the size they can take up.

/usr
This is the secondary hierarchy level for read-only user data. This will house most of the user utilities and applications. It is filled with several different files, such as:

- **/usr/bin:** binary files for user programs
- **/usr/sbin:** the system admins' binary files
- **/usr/lib:** libraries for /usr/bin or /usr/sbin
- **/usr/local:** Programs that have been installed from their sources
- **/usr/src:** the Linux kernel sources

The Process Architecture of Linux

Process architecture is the design that dictates the hierarchy of processes and systems when transforming any inputs to outputs in computing. While this sounds complicated to understand at a glance, hopefully, this subchapter will help you get through this process with ease.

The purpose of the process architecture

Within the Linux kernel are several subsystems, and the most important is the process scheduler. The purpose of the process scheduler is to control any access to the CPU, regardless of whether the access is via user process or from another kernel subsystem. This is all done by the process scheduler, which can itself be divided into four distinct modules as it interacts with the rest of the computer.

Linux processes

Commands issued to Linux trigger processes. When you insert a command into Linux, then, a new process begins. This process is assigned a 5-digit ID that allows the OS to track the processes—this will be known as the pid (process ID). While pids may be recycled, no two processes will share the same pid at the same time due to the pids being the process through which Linux is able to track the process in the first place.

This process is run one of two ways: In the foreground or the background. When in the foreground, where processes start by default, you are able to insert your input to the keyboard, and you get output on the screen.

However, while these processes are running in the foreground, you are unable to complete other processes as well. For this reason, sometimes, processes get booted to background processes, where they run in the background, with no access to keyboard input, until that input becomes required.

With it running in the background, other processes can be handled at the same time, meaning you can multitask until you are required to input further data. The process runs as one of three distinct types: Parent and child, zombie and orphan, or daemon processes. Each of these different process types function slightly differently.

- **Parent and child process:** This occurs when a process creates another knowhow. The created process is known as the child process while the parent process is the one that triggered the second.

- **Zombie and orphan process:** Upon finishing its function, the child process becomes terminated, and SIGCHLD, the signal from the interface to the parent process, informs the parent process of the termination of the child process. However, sometimes, the parent process is terminated before the child process terminates, creating a situation in which the child process is orphaned. The parent process still has an entry to the process table but is not functioning

- **Daemon process:** These processes are system-related and run in the background, most often running with permissions of root and waiting for processes that will work with them.

Process scheduler modules

The process schedule comes in four modules that will work together to organize the processes. These modules are:

- **The scheduling policy module:** This module judges which processes are granted access to the CPU, granting fair access to CPU to all processes.

- **The architecture-specific modules:** This is actually several modules—they are designed to share an interface that allows for the abstraction of details of any computer architecture. Their purpose is to communicate with the CPU in order to suspend or resume processes through knowing what information is needed to be preserved for processes and executing assembly codes that directly interact with whether a process with be suspended or resumed.

- **The architecture-independent module:** This module is the center of it all—it communicates first with the policy module to decide which process goes next, then tasks the architecture-specific schedulers to resume the right process. It then interacts with the memory manager to make sure that there is enough memory hardware available for the process to run effectively.

- **The system call interface module:** This module allows user processes to access only resources that are intentionally and explicitly exported by the kernel. This regulates the divide between user and kernel memory.

As pictured in the graphic below, the architecture-independent module is at the heart of this entire process and directly interacts with each of the other modules, allowing the entire process to run together effectively in a way that actually works. The scheduler essentially manages it all, with an entry for each process. The entire graphic encompasses what is known as the process scheduler.

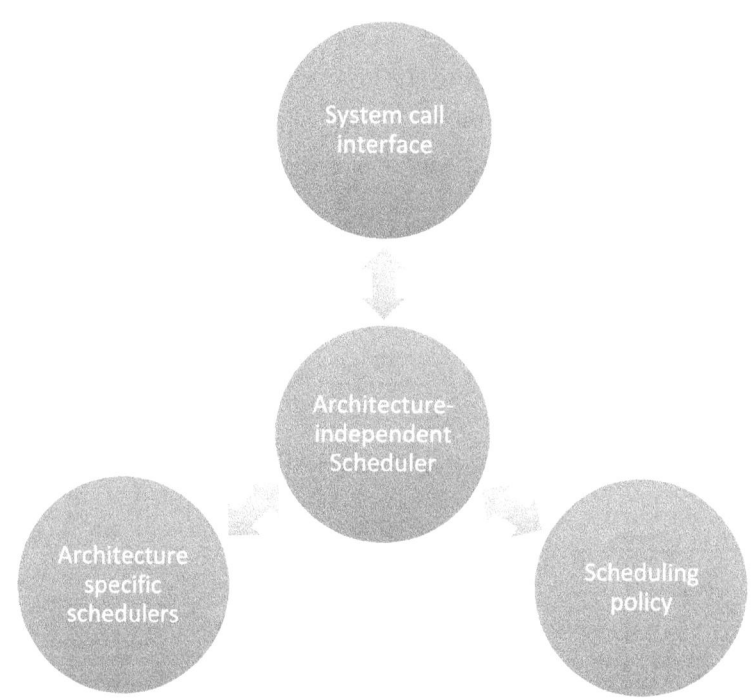

Chapter 1 Quiz

Congratulations! You have made it through Chapter 1. Try to answer these questions to ensure you understand the basics before moving on. The answer key will be on the page directly after this quiz.

1. What is the operating system?

    a. The person or people operating the system
    b. The program that controls the hardware
    c. The program that controls the software
    d. The program that controls the hardware and software
    e. All of the above
    f. None of the above

2. Why do you need to keep the kernel space separate from the user space?

    a. Because you don't want the user space to run out of memory
    b. Because you don't want to run out of space for the operating system
    c. Because you don't want the kernel space to accidentally damage files on the user face
    d. Because you don't want to mix personal and business files
    e. All of the above
    f. None of the above

3. **True or false: Unix came after Linux**

4. **True or false: Linux was built with Python**

5. How many times can a pid be reused?

    a. Never—it can only be used once
    b. A handful of times—so long as there are not two processes sharing the pid at one time
    c. Infinitely, so long as there are not two processes sharing the pid at one time
    d. All processes originating on one device share the same pid

Chapter 1 Answer Key

1. **D**. The operating system allows the user to control and interact with both the hardware and the software, but it is not the user him- or herself.

2. **B**. If the kernel were to run out of space for necessary functions, the system would crash, so keeping the memory split between kernel and user guarantees that there is always enough space for the kernel to function.

3. **False.** Linux was heavily influenced by Unix and Unix-influenced programs such as MINIX and GNU.

4. **False.** Linux was coded with C.

5. **C**. There is no limit to the number of times a pid can be reused, so long as there is never a current duplicate.

Chapter 2: Choose Your Distribution

So, you've made it to Chapter 2, congratulations! You have gotten through the background information that you will need to understand in order to proceed and have decided that you do, in fact, want to use Linux as your OS. Unfortunately, it is not as simple as just deciding to use Linux. Remember, Linux itself refers to the Linux kernel—the core of the operating system. From there, there are several other components, and while the core remains constant, your decisions on all of the other aspects of the OS, such as the GNU, the X server, and more, can all drastically alter your experience.

Some of the versions of Linux, known as Linux distributions, or more commonly shortened to "Linux distros," will be easy enough to hop right in to using, while others could be your worst nightmare immediately upon installing it, such as Gentoo, which requires all programs, including the kernel, to be built from source.

This chapter will guide you through understanding what a Linux distribution is, how to decide which distribution will be right for you and your usage, and then provide you with a brief overview of ten of the most common distributions you can find.

What is a Linux Distribution?

When you think of other operating systems, you would most likely think of Windows or macOS—two of the most commonly known and used operating systems out there. These are built from the ground up by a single company with incremental upgrades and changes, and because of that, you get distinct versions.

You have Windows XP, Windows 7, Windows, 8, Windows 10, etc. with the latest version of Windows (Windows 10 at the time of writing this book), being the most up-to-date and supported. If you want to go out and buy Windows for your computer right now through Microsoft, your choice is to get Windows 10. Of course, you can get other, older editions through other sources, but they are not actively supported, nor are they going to always be updated for security. At a certain point, companies stop rolling out support for their older, more obsolete software.

Unlike Windows or macOS, however, Linux is not created by a single company. Linux can be mixed and matched. So long as you have all of the right components together to create a complete OS, you can put it together. This means that you can, in fact, create an entire OS more or less from scratch, using the Linux kernel as your base, though that would be quite time-consuming, and you would have to put in some work to configure everything to work together. Alternatively, you can seek out Linux distributions.

The Linux distribution is essentially everything all neatly packaged together for you. It takes all of the open-source information you would otherwise need to seek out on your own and puts it together into a single OS, not unlike what you would receive when purchasing licenses to use Windows or macOS. They decide which desktops you will have, which programs will be loaded up by default, and more, typically with a layer of their own custom interface. Of course, this also implies that there will be a nearly infinite number of different distributions available to you, all of which can provide all sorts of different features. This is why it is important for you to do your research before choosing one.

How to Choose the Right Distribution for You

Now comes the hard part—figuring out which distribution will be right for you. As you read through the rest of this chapter, consider the questions that will be asked here. What are you installing the OS on? What is the purpose of the OS? Do you have any experience? What kind of software availability to you want or need? What kind of desktop interface do you want? How often do you need updates?

All of these are incredibly important questions to keep in mind. If you are not careful, you could end up with a version of Linux that you do not actually want, or cannot actually make use of.

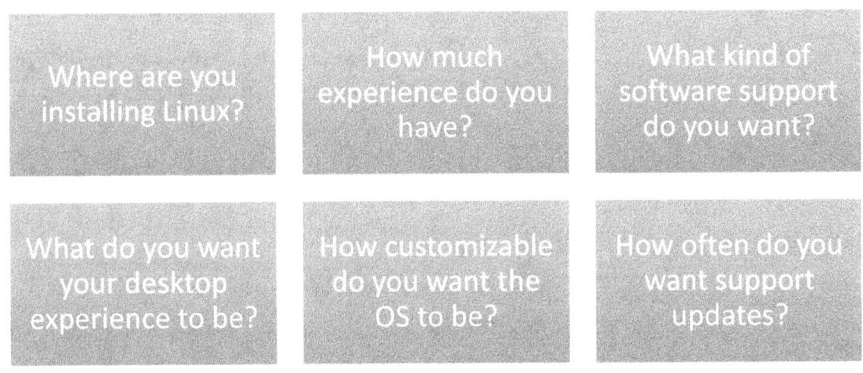

As you read through each of the ten distributions that are provided to you, you will be provided with a brief overview of the OS itself, whether it is suited for beginners or those with plenty of experience, how regularly it is updated, and how compatible it is. You will need to choose one that works best for you.

Ubuntu

The first distribution we will consider is Ubuntu. Launched in 2004, it is now officially available in three different versions: Desktop, Server, and Core. Each of these editions can be run on a computer or in a virtual machine, making this a popular choice in OS for cloud computing, especially thanks to its support for OpenStack. In fact, Linux is the most popular desktop Linux distribution currently available. Originally based on Debian sid, commonly referred to as the unstable distribution, thanks to its lack of stability. While Debian sid was unstable, Ubuntu has been built intentionally, avoiding the mistakes made within sid or other similar projects. In doing so, it created a web-based infrastructure, bug-reporting, and professional creation.

This particular form of Linux utilizes GNOME, Firefox, and LibreOffice by default, all updated, and it utilizes regular, predictable support updates. Ultimately, the creation was a well-formed OS that also includes a migration assistant for those transferring from Windows, support for latest tech, and it is compatible with ATI and NVIDIA graphics cards.

Difficulty rating: Good for beginners

Long-term support: Regularly updated distributions every 6 months with long term support releases as well.

Pros:

- Regular updates on fixed cycle and support periods
- Long-term support variants come with 5 years of updates for security
- Beginner-friendly
- Widely-used, meaning there is plenty of advice, opinions, and support available online

Cons

- Incompatible with Debian
- Regular updates often come with major changes that may be annoying to some
- Variants that are not LTS only have 9 months of security support

Linux Mint

Linux Mint is a distribution that is based on Ubuntu. This distribution was first launched in 2006, just two years after the release of Ubuntu. This particular form was created by Clement Lefebvre, a French-born IT specialist who resided in Ireland at the time of creation. He had originally been maintaining a website that provided help and guides to people new to Linux, and during his time maintaining this site, he came up with an idea to develop his own Linux distribution in order to address several drawbacks present with other mainstream versions of Linux.

Though commonly referred to as "Ubuntu done right," Linux Mint is more than just Ubuntu with a refresh—it includes several tools designed to enhance the Linux Mint experience, often aptly named with "mint," such as mintDesktop, mintMenu, mintUpdate, and more. The mint tools are designed to be more usable, and greatly increase the ease of use, making this one of the easiest forms of Linux to pick up thanks to the emphasis on user-friendliness.

One of the biggest draws to Linux Mint is the fact that the developers are always ready and happy to implement good suggestions that will help better the program.

Difficulty rating: Good for beginners

Long-term support: Not on a fixed schedule, but is regularly updated, especially shortly after each of Ubuntu's LTS releases.

Pros:

- mint tools designed for the OS
- User-friendly
- Includes multimedia codecs
- Open to the requests and suggestions of the users

Cons:

- No security advisories
- Not predictably updated

MX Linux

MX Linux has a bit of a history to it. Originally known as MEPIS Linux, a Debian-based distribution meant for both personal and professional purpose desktops, featured several cutting-edge features at the time of its creation. However, despite this cutting-edge availability, MEPIS Linux eventually was subject to discontinuation. Its users, however, were not to be deterred. Merging MEPIS with another Debian-based distribution known as antiX resulted in what is known now as MX Linux. This is based on Debian's stable branch, with primary components from both the antiX and MEPIS communities. In particular, it utilizes the Xfce desktop along with a vertical panel on the side instead of the common horizontal control panel across the bottom of most computers. Overall, this distribution is recognized as one that offers plenty of modern apps that are occasionally updated, along with a stable base, allowing for the creation of good, reliable performance without losing those features that people want most.

In particular, MX Linux is recognized for its MX-Tools—a series of graphical administration utilities that allow for ready access to several functions, such as managing the user accounts on that system, installing codecs, and utilizing and installing software packages.

Difficulty rating: Good for beginners

Long-term support: Features occasional updates through backports

Pros:

- Immediate support for graphics drivers, codecs, and browser plugins allow for near-instant startup out of the box
- Stable
- Updated periodically
- Convenient features

Cons

- Simple and dated appearance
- The installer and other configuration tools may take some time to adjust to

openSUSE

Dating back to 1992, openSUSE came about when four German Linux enthusiasts launched it. Thomas Fehr, Roland Dyroff, Hubert Mantel, and Burchard Steinbild started out selling floppy disks with the German edition of Slackware but quickly created their own program: SuSE (Software und System Entwicklung, or software and system development). In 1996, SuSE Linux became its own distribution, and over time, more and more features were adopted, such as the RPM package management tool, a graphical system administration tool designed for usability, and more.

They released frequently, kept fantastic documentation, and made their product readily available, and SuSE Linux grew more and more popular.

In 2003, it was acquired by Novell, INC, and eventually transferred to Attachmate in 2010. These exchanges in ownership led to major changes in development, and eventually, the change in name from SuSE to openSUSE. Despite the constant changes, however, it is readily available for free. You can find openSUSE in two primary editions. Leap grants users a platform that is stable and has several years of support.

Tumbleweed, on the other hand, uses a rolling release environment, and this is made smooth by the easy configuration and automated filesystem snapshots and boot environments.

Difficulty rating: Good for beginners with some experience

Long-term support: Plenty of support offered

Pros	Cons
• Configuration tool is comprehensive	• Bloated and heavy desktop setup
• Plenty of software packages	• Graphical utilities are slow
• Fantastic website infrastructure	
• Plenty of printed documentation and support	
• Btrfs with boot environments	

Fedora

Fedora itself was not announced and revealed until 2004, though its roots back to 1995 with Red Hat Linux, which was launched by Bob Young and Marc Ewing. Their product was released and updated several times, and in 1997, it added the RPM package management system, along with several other advanced features, which quickly shot Red Hat to popularity, eventually even surpassing Slackware Linux as the most widely-used distribution at the time. In 2003, after Red Hat Linux 9 was released, the company made some significant changes, keeping Red Hat trademarked as commercial use and then also adding in Fedora Core.

Eventually named just Fedora, this system is sponsored by Red Hat but primarily oriented toward the Linux hobbyist. Despite initial reservations, it was quickly accepted and once again skyrocketed back to its status as one of the favorites. This is commonly deemed one of the more innovative of the options available these days. Fedora has led the way in contributions to Linux as a whole and has made use of several enterprise-level features. However, it runs into some downsides as well—it requires some technical knowhow to really make good use of it, meaning that it is still a better product for the hobbyists who enjoy tinkering rather than someone trying to learn.

Difficulty rating: Intermediate

Long-term support: Regularly updated

Pros:

- Innovative and Secure
- Massive number of supported packages
- Strongly aligned with free software philosophy

Cons

- Enterprise rather than desktop features and usability
- Bleeding-edge features can sometimes be alienating to those who are less familiar with the system
- Requires a bit more finesse with Linux in general

Debian GNU/Linux

Announced in 1993, this was designed to become a non-commercial project completed through volunteer work of hundreds of developers. Most people thought it would fail—after all, how could hundreds of developers code for free in their spare time and create something cohesive? Nevertheless, the project was successful, and Debian became the largest Linux distribution within a decade.

It encompassed 1,000 volunteer developers' work, with nearly 50,000 binary packages for eight different processor architectures. From this effort came more than 120 other distributions based on Debian. No other Linux-based OS comes close to these numbers. Debian exists in four main branches in several different developmental stages—"Experimental," "Unstable," also regularly known as sid, "Testing," and "Stable." Thanks to this process, it is recognized to have quite intensive levels of quality control, and Debian has earned recognition as one of the best-established, tested, and bug-free distributions you can find. Of course, the development process does have some down sides.

In particular, the stable releases only come out every few years, and because they go through so much testing, they are not particularly competitive.

Difficulty rating: Good for beginners with some experience

Long-term support: Support is there, but new stable releases only come out every few years

Pros	Cons
• Quite stable	• Newer stable software is usually not as cutting-edge due to the development
• Fantastic quality control	
• More than 30,000 software packages	• Conservative due to the several processor architectures being supported
• Recognizes and supports more processor architectures than other distributions	

Arch Linux

Designed for simple usability in 2002 by Judd Vinet, it was initially designed to be used for intermediate-to-advanced users of Linux who were already familiar with the OS. It did eventually gain popularity when promoted as a "rolling-release" distribution, meaning that it would only need the initial install to get it going.

From there, all that would be needed to keep the installation up to date was a monthly snapshot of install media to refresh the software. This was made possible by the package manager known as Pacman. It is also able to install software packages from source code, making it incredibly efficient, especially in tandem with its ability to simply pack up binary packages and the constantly increasing repository of tested software packages. Despite its initial design for users with experience, thanks to the Arch Linux Handbook, along with all of the documentation of usage, it now allows for users with less experience with Linux to install, understand, and utilize it, and with the powerful tools it boasts, this distribution can be customized endlessly.

However, the rolling-release can cause problems, especially in the case of human error. Even a slight mishap can lead to a system that no longer boots after upgrading. This means that, though there is plenty of information out there, this is still a system that will require some technical knowhow and experience to fix any problems that may arise.

Difficulty rating: Intermediate—need some experience to really use this well.

Long-term support: Regular rolling updates

Pros

- Fantastic software management structure
- Incredibly customizable with endless possibilities
- Plenty of online documentation and guidance available

Cons

- Can be difficult to catch on when a beginner
- Occasional breakdowns occur
- Breakdowns require experience to handle and fix

Slackware

Created in 1992, Slackware is the oldest Linux distribution that is still surviving. It was forked from a discontinued project and initially was released on 24 separate floppy disks and built upon Linux kernel verson 0.99pl11-alpha. It rose to popularity among the Linux distributions available, and by 1995, it is believed to have held a massive 80% of Linux installations. However, as newer, an , and user-friendly options arrived on the market, the population of Slackware quickly declined. Despite the declination in popularity, it is still alive and kicking, and is enjoyed by those who are on the more technologically capable side.

Because it is not particularly customizable, it is quite clean and technical. It primarily utilizes a text-based system installer, and the package management system is quite outdated and primitive compared to more modern options available. However, because it is so simple and basic, it is also one of the cleanest of the Linux distributions you can get today, making it incredibly stable. Without enhancements, the chances of accidentally introducing a bug to the system are slim. Between its reliability and lack of bugs, Slackware Linux is quickly becoming a core system—one that serves as the foundation for other software as opposed to complete distribution. Thought not competitive by any means at this point, it is still utilized by some today.

Difficulty rating: Advanced

Long-term support: Maintained, but not patched or customized

Pros

- Stable and mostly bug-free
- Adheres to Unix principles
- Largely unchanged from initial conceptualization

Cons

- Very conservative—no room for customizability
- Requires a lot of work to be used as modern desktop
- The upgrade procedure is difficult
- No official security support or updates

Gentoo

Despite being the butt of several jokes floating around the internet, Gentoo is a valid option for people who know what they are doing. This particular distribution is quick and flexible while also entirely free. It is designed in particular for people with plenty of IT knowledge, such as developers and network professionals.

It is built with a source-based package management system known as Portage—a Python-based true ports system that comes with several advanced features of its own that can make Gentoo an attractive prospect to those who understand how to use it.

Originally created in 2000 by Daniel Robbins with a vision of creating a meta-distribution without needing any pre-compiled binary packages. He certainly succeeded—when you install Gentoo, you set up a system with the bare minimum to boot up, and from there, you must program it yourself. The system itself is incredibly customizable, and you are free to add and remove from it to make it work for you. Thanks to this, it is well-known for the flexibility it grants to those who choose to use it.

They are able to create a wide range of experiences, and because of this, Gentoo can be found at the heart of several other projects, such as creating the foundation for Google's Chrome OS.

Difficulty rating: Advanced

Long-term support: Regular releases

Pros

- Flexible and customizable
- Can use several different compile-time configurations
- Can use several init systems
- Can run on several different architectures

Cons

- Requires a high level of knowledge to get started
- Takes longer to set up
- The process to upgrade packages through source can be lengthy

CentOS

Released in 2003, this is a community project that endeavored to rebuild source code for Red Hat Enterprise Linux into something that could be readily installed with regular security updates for everything included. Effectively, this makes CentOS a clone of Red Hat Enterprise Linux (RHEL), with the one difference between them being branding. Despite the fact that CentOS is a clone, there does not seem to be any real conflict between the two.

CentOS is deemed to be reliable as a server distribution—thanks to the utilization of the stable Linux kernel and software packages of RHEL. It has been deemed to be a reliable and free alternative to other server products that are available today, especially for those who are already quite experienced with Linux as a whole. These people find little difficulty in administrating the distribution.

CentOS is also usable for enterprise desktops as well—if you need something stable and reliable, with a preference for the support over cutting-edge software, this is the OS for you. Of course, if you do care about up-to-date and cutting-edge software, you may prefer to look elsewhere, as the updates to CentOS are a bit spaced out compared to some of the other options on the market.

Difficulty rating: Beginners with some experience

Long-term support: Regular updates are rolled out every 9-12 months, and new releases come out every 2-3 years

Pros

- Brings stability and reliability to the table
- Free software
- 7+ years of security updates
- Well-tested

Cons

- Does not utilize the most up-to-date technology
- Releases and updates do not always live up to their promises

Chapter 2 Quiz

Congratulations! You have made it through Chapter 2. Do you have an idea of which distribution you would like to try at this point? Try to answer these questions to ensure you understand the fundamental information before moving on to Chapter 3. The answer key will be on the page directly after this quiz.

1. What is a Linux distribution?

    a. A book that tells you how to install Linux
    b. A specific operating system programmed around the Linux kernel
    c. The newest Linux hardware
    d. All of the above
    e. None of the above

2. True or false: All Linux distributions are constantly changing

3. When choosing the distribution that is right for you, which features should you consider?

    a. User-friendliness and your own competency
    b. How well it serves your own needs
    c. The built in software
    d. Whether you like the mascot
    e. a, b, and c
    f. a, b, and d

4. True or false: Gentoo is great for beginners

5. True or false: Ubuntu is great for beginners

Chapter 2 Answer Key

1. **B:** The distribution refers to the specific operating system program that you are using

2. **False:** Several distributions, such as Slackware, do not change much or have not changed in years.

3. **E:** While liking the mascot may be nice, it does not determine how well a program may meet your needs

4. **False:** Gentoo requires nearly constant programming to get it functioning at all.

5. **True:** Ubuntu is incredibly easy to get started with and is designed to be user-friendly.

Chapter 3: Install Linux

At this point, you should be ready to install Linux. However, you have yet another decision to make. Will you install your distribution on a virtual machine, or will you be running it on hardware? Even if you choose to install on hardware, will you run it as your primary OS, or will you create a partition for your chosen distribution?

If you are a beginner to looking into operating systems, this may seem intimidating, but try not to worry. This chapter will guide you through the basics of installing Linux on your device. When you are able to load up several different operating systems on one machine, you are able to toggle between them. This means that you can take advantage of everything your computer potentially has to offer through choosing exactly the software that will do whatever it is that you need to be done. What you will get from this chapter, however, will be a solid foundation on what a virtual machine is and why you may choose to use them. You will be guided through the installation of Linux on your physical computer through the use of a USB drive, step-by-step. Then, you will be guided through the creation of a virtual machine on your machine running Windows, allowing you to effectively run an instance of Linux within the virtual machine itself. Lastly, you will be guided through the installation of Linux on a virtual machine on a computer that is currently running macOS. By the end of this chapter, you should feel comfortable with the idea of installing Linux onto your own device, whether you choose to install it on the physical machine itself or whether you prefer instead to run a virtual machine within the OS of your choice.

What is a Virtual Machine?

A virtual machine is an app on your computer that allows you to run an instance of an operating system within it.

This allows you to effectively be running your particular machine's native OS while simultaneously using another OS entirely within a window on your desktop. Virtual machines are not Linux-specific—you can run a macOS virtual machine on a Windows or Linux device, run Windows on a macOS or Linux device, or run Linus on a Windows or macOS device.

Effectively, when using a virtual machine, the app you are running functions as its own separate computer apart from the device that it is running on. The application creates the ability to run even virtual hardware devices. This means that your computer thinks that it is running on its own individual computer, monitoring its own processes, and using virtual hardware.

Unlike trying to run two operating systems on your computer, which requires partitioning, the virtual machine instead crates a virtual hard drive. This is a file that will be stored on your actual hard drive—this large file, typically multi-gigabytes, gets presented to the virtual machine as a hard drive, allowing you to bypass needing to create any sort of partition or anything else that may become complicated with the hard drive. Do keep in mind that, while a virtual machine is great for creating virtual instances of an OS for your usage, it is notably slower than running a proper OS. Because of the extra steps that go into supporting the virtual machine, it does have some further processing power required. This means that a virtual machine is most likely not your best way to be playing games of any sort. As a major pro, however, the only limit to how many virtual machines you can have installed is only limited by the amount of physical hard drive space you have available to you. If you have enough room, you can continue to add more installations of several other operating systems.

However, you must keep in mind that each of these installations will take up at least several gigabytes of space within your hard drive. You can also choose to run several virtual machines at the same time, though again, you will find that the upper limit is your physical hardware. Your virtual machines will each need access to some of your processor, RAM, and other resources, meaning that the more you are actively trying to use at any given time, the weaker the running will most likely be. There are several reasons that someone may choose to run a virtual machine.

For some, this could be done just to mess with. If you are particularly interested in computers and how they work, you may choose to use a virtual machine to play around in other operating systems that you are not actively running as your primary OS. This means that you can mess around with a new OS before deciding if you really want to install it physically, allowing you to, for example, play with several different Linux distributions before you chose which you prefer to use.

Other people may find that they have very specific needs from time to time that requires a limited app that is only available with a specific OS. For example, if you are running Linux, but need an application that was primarily contained within Windows XP, you could choose to run Windows XP on a virtual machine to make use of that specific app.

One other common reason that people use virtual machines is the fact that the virtual machine is sandboxed. This means that it is all contained within the virtual machine itself, so there is nothing that you can do within the virtual machine that puts the rest of your system at risk. Like a sandbox and its sides to contain it, the virtual machine is entirely sequestered within the hard drive and will not be impacted by whatever it is that you have chosen to do within it. This means that you can test apps that are being developed in a safe space without worrying about the repercussions that would occur if the entire system failed.

Benefits of the Virtual Machine

Allows for toying with and testing of new operating systems	Allows for the use of apps that are otherwise unavailable to the native OS.	It is sandboxed, meaning that anything done within the virtual machine is separate from everything else.

Installing Linux on Physical Hardware

Before it is time to worry about the virtual machine, however, you will first learn how to install Linux on physical hardware. When using this process, you are creating the option to install Linux on your computer as a separate partition. This means that you will have two (or more) operating systems on your machine. This process will be given to you step by step.

Step 1: Downloading the Linux distribution

Did you choose out distribution in the previous chapter? If so, this is what you will be searching. If you have not yet decided which you prefer to use, you will need to spend the time making your decision. If you are reading this book, you are most likely new to Linux as a whole, and because of this, you will find that you are best served by a lightweight distribution that will be a bit more user-friendly, such as Ubuntu or Linux Mint. Of course, you can also choose to challenge yourself and go for something a bit more intensive if you so choose. Before beginning, also make sure that you have a CD or a USB drive that you can use for the installation. Because CD drives are largely becoming obsolete in many consumer-grade products, the USB is most likely going to be the most readily-accessible form for any computer.

Once you have chosen the distribution that you will use, you must download it. You can find the distro free to download in an ISO format. This is an archive file that has an identical copy of data that was found on a disc and is the most common format to distribute Linux. The identical copy is known as the image and is what you are seeking to copy in order to install the software.

1. Download the ISO for the distribution of Linux you have chosen on the distribution's website.
2. Prepare the USB to become bootable with a program such as Rufus.
3. Install an image burning program such as Pen Drive Linux or UNetBootin.
4. Load image onto the formatted USB.

Step 2: Booting into the live USB

Now, you are tasked with loading into the live USB in the first place. Most computers will set to boot, starting with the hard drive, so you will need to make some changes to the default booting order before it makes the necessary changes. This process is not as intimidating as it sounds—all you need to do is reboot the computer, enter the boot menu, and choose the source that you would like your computer to boot from. Sometimes, the boot menu is hidden from view, but it is still accessible. In these situations, you will need to access the BIOS menu in order to gain access to the boot menu, which can be done at the splash screen. The command necessary to load into the BIOS menu should be displayed in one of the bottom corners on the splash screen.

1. Reboot the computer
2. As the computer reboots, press the key to trigger the boot menu. You should see the necessary key in the corner of the splash screen—the screen where the manufacturer's logo is displayed during the initial startup. Common keys to access the boot menu are F12 or Del.
    a. If you are using Windows 8, try holding the Shift key while clicking restart. This triggers the computer to boot with the Advanced Startup Options, allowing you to make the decision.
3. When in the boot menu, select the live USB or CD that you are using to load up Linux. Upon choosing your method, save and exit the boot menu or BIOS. Your machine should continue with the booting process with your selected settings.

Step 3: Try Linux before installing (optional)

Trying the version of Linux that you are in the process of installing is optional, but strongly recommended if you are not yet familiar with Linux or you are unsure which version to install. Your live USB should allow you to launch what is referred to as a live environment, allowing you to test it prior to making any sort of changes. While you will be unable to create files during this stage, you will be free to navigate the system and experience the interface to make an informed decision before spending the time to install and format.

Step 4: Starting installation

The installation process itself is quite simple. From the boot menu, you will have the option to install rather than launch. At this point, your machine will handle the bulk of the work, but you will be prompted to configure basic options, such as the language that you will be using with the OS, the keyboard layout, and the time zone you are in.

Step 5: Creating a user

At this point, you will be prompted to create the login information for your OS. You will insert your name, your computer's name, the username that you are choosing for this instance, and a password for logging in and confirming that you are authorized to perform any administrative tasks.

Step 6: Creating the partition (optional)

If Linux is your primary OS, you can skip this step. However, if you are running multiple operating systems on your machine, you will need to separate out a partition specifically for your version of Linux. The partition is the portion that has been formatted in the way that the specific OS requires, allowing for the OS to run as intended.

Some more beginner-friendly distributions, such as Ubuntu, will format the partition on their own, though you can adjust the size manually. Keep in mind that most installations will need at least 20 GB, so you must make sure that whatever partition you set will accommodate the OS *and* any other files and programs that will be stored within it. Sometimes, the installation process will not automatically configure the automatic partition, and when this happens, you must make sure that the partition is in the format Ext4.

Step 7: Booting Linux

When the installation finishes, it will automatically prompt you to reboot. Upon booting, you will see a different screen. This will pull up the bootloader, which will prompt you to pick the distribution you are installing. One of the more likely bootloaders that you will encounter is GNU GRUB.

Of course, if you have opted to skip the partition stage and load your Linux distro as your only OS, you will likely not see this screen automatically. As with before, you can trigger the bootloader by pressing the Shift key immediately after the manufacturer splash screen loads.

Step 8: Checking hardware

While most hardware should be fine immediately after installation, you may find that some of the hardware you are using will require you to download some drivers. In particular, graphics cards are notorious for requiring extra drivers. You can usually find some sort of open source driver to get the job done, but if you want to really optimize your GPU, you will need to get the proper drivers from the manufacturer.

Step 9: Using Linux

At this point, your installation should be complete, and your hardware should be functioning. At this point, you are ready to begin using your new OS! You may choose to go download programs that will allow you to optimize your usage of the program, or you can go on your way using it.

Installing Linux on Virtual Machines on Windows 10

Sometimes, the method you will be using to install Linux will utilize a virtual machine. In particular, you may choose to use a virtual machine to sandbox software in order to ensure that you do not damage any of the files on your primary OS. You may also wish to mess around in the operating system a bit more before taking the plunge and installing it. Luckily, using a virtual machine on Windows does not need to be difficult. 64-bit versions of Windows 10 Pro, Enterprise, or Education already are preloaded with a proprietary virtual machine known as Hyper-V, meaning that you will not need to go out of your way to get more software. If you do not have Hyper-V already, you will need to find a VM program. A free option that you can use is Oracle VM VirtualBox.

Step 1: Installing the virtual machine

Start by verifying that you already have a virtual machine installed. Do this by searching for "Hyper-V" on your computer under Windows features. You should see boxes on the left-hand side. When you check those boxes next to the files, you are turning files on and off. Click to enable Hyper-V if you can find it on your computer. Upon installation, you will need to reboot. If you do not have Hyper-V, search for another VM program that you seem to like online and install it.

Step 2: Setting up the virtual machine

At this stage, you must make sure that you have enough hard drive space available for the OS and files of your choice, and you will need the ISO file you intend to use. As in the previous version, the ISO can be downloaded from the distributor.

If you are using Hyper-V, searching for Hyper-V Quick Create will give you a sort of shortcut to ensuring that everything is set up as necessary.

All you will need to do is follow the prompts on the screen within the program, selecting your ISO file if you do not wish to use one of the provided ones.

Without Hyper-V, you will find the process to be slightly less streamlined, but still quite manageable overall. Most virtualization software will be quite similar—it will be a matter of preference and availability to determine which you prefer.

1. Upon launching VirtualBox, you will see an empty menu. From there, you will need to click on the NEW icon in the top left of the program's window. You will then name the VM and then select which kind of OS you will be using.

2. Next, you need to allocate memory to the VM, providing it with the necessary resources. Typically, the best bet is to going to be to take the recommended amount and then click next.

3. The next prompt you will see will ask if you want to add a virtual drive. Agree to this, click Create, and select VDI on the list. VDI stands for the virtual disk image. Choose the Fixed Size option on the next page. At the end, you will be asked to name the drive you are using and then confirm the size.

4. Click create, and the virtual drive has been created.

Step 3: Installing the OS

At this point, it is time to install your chosen distribution of Linux. Within the VirtualBox window, select the Start arrow. It should open up a window that will be titled Select startup disk. Click the folder on the right, next to the drop-down menu, and here, you can select the ISO file for your distribution. From there, all you do is click Start, and the OS should be installed.

Step 4: Shutting down the virtual machine

When you get to the point where you are done with the machine, resist the urge to just click out of the window. Instead, click on the File menu and select the option to close while selecting 'Save the machine state.' This ensures that you will keep the information within the virtual machine.

Installing Linux on Virtual Machines on macOS High Sierra

At the time of writing this book, the current macOS is High Sierra. Installing Linux through a virtual machine on High Sierra is largely similar to how you would go through the process on Windows. Considering, at this point, you have been guided through the most difficult processes, this will be the shortest guide of them all. All you will be doing that is new within this chapter is installing VirtualBox on the macOS. From there, you can follow the steps detailed in the previous subchapter.

Step 1: Run VirtualBox

1. Start by running the VirtualBox installer. You may see a warning that that macOS does not allow unsecure system extensions. Just click 'Next' and keep going.
2. At the end of the installation, it will fail. Don't worry about the failure; just keep following this tutorial.

3. Go to System Preferences > Security & Privacy. At the bottom, there should be a prompt that says that the system software was blocked. At the bottom left corner of the window, click on the lock. It will ask you to put in your password. Do so and then click 'Allow' next to the message telling you that the program was blocked from loading.

4. Reload the VirtualBox installer. It should go through this time.

At this point, the process is largely the same as opening a VM in Windows. The only differing point between the two was the installation process.

Chapter 3 Quiz

Congratulations! You have made it through Chapter 3. At this point, you should be prepared to load up Linux on your own devices. Try to answer these questions to ensure you understand the basics before moving on to Chapter 4. The answer key will be on the page directly after this quiz.

1. Which tools are necessary to install Linux (either on hardware or on a virtual machine)?
    a. ISO file
    b. USB drive
    c. Virtualbox
    d. A and C
    e. All of the above
    f. None of the above

2. What is necessary to run several operating systems on the same system?
    a. Virtualbox
    b. A USB drive
    c. A partition in the hard drive
    d. A computer with two hard drives
    e. All of the above
    f. None of the above

3. What is a virtual machine?
    a. A computer capable of running operating systems within operating systems at the same time
    b. A way to keep an OS partitioned away from the other parts of the computer's OS
    c. A method that can be used to test software
    d. All of the above
    e. None of the above

4. True or false: You need a virtual machine if you want to run Linux

5. True or false: the USB drive that you will load the ISO onto will be ready out of the box

Chapter 3 Answer Key

1. **A:** The only listed component that is necessary to run Linux is the ISO file that is used to distribute the OS. The USB drive can be bypassed when installing on a virtual machine, and Virtualbox can be bypassed when installing on hardware with a USB.

2. **C:** The only necessary component listed is the partitions between operating systems. Virtualbox is one specific virtual machine, but there are several that will work in its place, the USB drive is not necessary, and you do not have to have two hard drives—the whole point of the virtual machine is to partition a single hard drive to accommodate several operating systems.

3. **D**

4. **False:** You can install Linux onto the hardware, bypassing the need for a virtual machine.

5. **False:** You must format the USB drive to be ready to accommodate the ISO.

Chapter 4: Linux Shell

With Linux freshly installed, it is time to begin interacting with your new OS. This is primarily done through what is known as a shell. The shell allows you to interact with the operating system, which at this point, you should understand is crucial for the functioning of your computer. Your operating system consists of several layers: at one end, you have the kernel, which is how the OS interacts with the hardware of the computer, and on the other end of the process, you have the shell, which the user interacts with.

Stop and consider this graphic for a moment: Note how the hardware is at heart. From there, you have the kernel that surrounds the hardware, and the shell that engulfs the kernel. This allows you to sort of see the hierarchy—you cannot access the innermost levels without first going through the external levels.

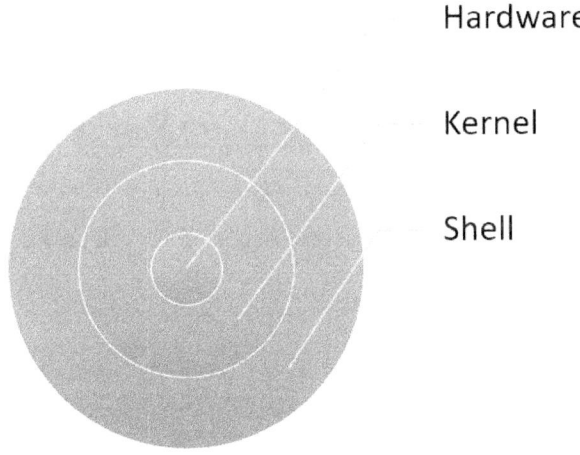

Within this chapter, you will learn what the shell is as a system, as well as what its primary functions are. You will learn how to access the shell through the terminal. You will be guided through shell scripting, as well as be provided with basic command line editing that you need to know in order to interact with the shell. Lastly, you will be walked through the types of shells available.

What is Shell?

Computers primarily operate on a binary—this is the usage of 1s and 0s to represent whether a switch is on or off. However, if you were asked to put your input into your system via binary, you would find yourself spending far longer than necessary trying to translate and input your code. This is where the shell comes in. Thanks to the shell, you do not have to master binary. The shell acts as the translator between human-friendly commands written in English and then translates them into something usable by the kernel. In translating everything for the kernel, you are free to memorize commands that are far simpler and more manageable. This also allows you to input your commands via a keyboard.

Overall, the shell has several key features, such as:

- **It is a user program:** It is an environment that is designed to accommodate human user interactions

- **It is a command language interpreter (CLI):** It receives and executes a command from standard input, such as a keyboard, without the need for the memorization and translation of difficult program languages such as binary.

- **It is automatic:** As soon as you open a terminal, the shell will begin functioning

- **It works with the kernel:** Though it is not a part of the kernel, it does work in tandem with the kernel in order to allow for the execution of programs, creation of files, or completion of any necessary commands.

- **It is versatile:** There are several different shells available for Linux, which will complete the same job, though they use different syntax and have varying built-in functions.

Gaining Access to the Shell

When you are interacting with a shell, there are several different methods through which you can use. The most common accesses to the Shell include the terminal and a secure shell connection. These will come with varying degrees of permissions and abilities. Most commonly, you will find that you are interacting with Bash, though sometimes, you may encounter other forms. Nevertheless, understanding how to access the shell is necessary.

Installing Bash on Windows

This section will require you to install Bash through the Git for Windows installer. It is providing straightforward instructions to you that may not seem particularly informative until you have the screen in front of you.

Nevertheless, return to this section when you are ready to install Bash if you want the quickest way to do so.

1. Terminal access to shell requires you to first install Bash. This is quite simple—download the Git for Windows installer. When running the installer, click on the run, and then on the next five screens, you will click "Next."

2. When presented with the option, select "Git from the command line and also from 3rd party software" and then click "Next." This selection will allow you to access via command line, which is what you need. If you mess this step up or miss the selection you need, restart the installer and change the options accordingly.

3. Click "Next again."

4. Select "Checkout Windows-style, commit Unix-style line endings" and then click "Next" again.

5. On the next screen, select the second option. You should select "Use Windows' default console window" and click "Next."

6. Click "Next" once more.

7. Install.

8. When the install has completed, select "Finish."

This should leave you with Git and Bash available. Bash is the default shell used in macOS X and in most forms of Linux, so you will not need to go through this process if you have one of those operating systems already installed on your computer.

What is the terminal?

A terminal is the CLI used to access Bash. As with the shell itself, Linux and Mac users will already have a terminal program installed.

You have also installed your own terminal access in the previous section if you used Git for Windows installer—Git is the commonly used terminal for Windows users. The terminal will be the way that you are accessing your computer. When you use Bash within the terminal, you are able to perform far more tasks than you have ever had to do before on your computer. This will also allow for the performance of several other tasks in an efficient manner, such as monitoring the current working directory, changing directories, creating new directories, and more.

Terminal access to shell

When you are ready to access Bash, you must use the right program for the program you are using. In OS X, it is usually referred to as Terminal. In Windows, it is Git Bash. In Linux, it is typically just referred to as Bash.

When trying to access your shell within Linux, the easiest way to do so is to run a terminal emulator. There are several terminal emulators available to you—these are programs that will emulate the terminal hardware that is typically used in Unix. They are then mimicked and utilized within Linux, being presented as a window for you to access and interact with. Upon accessing the emulator, you should have options to configure the terminal, allowing you to change the text and colors or other personal settings.

Most of the time, GNOME is available, especially if you are running Bash, though others also exist. Some other commonly used terminal emulators include xterm, Konsole, and LXDE.

GNOME can be found within the applications menu. Running it should bring up the terminal for you, which you can then begin to interact with. When you interact with the terminal, you will enter your commands, and hitting the Enter button on your keyboard should trigger it to send.

When you are in the terminal, there are several commands that will be critical for you to know, which will be discussed in Chapter 5. Before beginning, please recognize that your terminal will display the dollar sign ($) when it is waiting for input. Other shells may use a different character, but if you are working within Bash, it will be the $. This will let you know that you should insert your own commands.

Secure shell connection

Sometimes, there is a need to connect to shell accounts on a remote server. So long as the server that you wish to access is running the proper SSHD server software that will be able to manage and accept any connections, you should be able to use what is referred to as an SSH program. These grant a remote connection. When you have established a secure SH connection, the shell session will begin, and you will have the ability to control the server via typed commands on your local computer. This has several uses, but most commonly, it is utilized by network and system administrators. If you have a need for a secure method to remotely manage a computer, you will find SSH to be quite beneficial to you. In order to create the SSH connection, there are two necessary components: The client and the server-side component. The client is the application that you will use on your computer. You will use the client to connect to the other computer or server that you wish to control. The client then uses the information provided to initiate a connection. Through the verification of credentials, an encrypted connection is created.

The server must have a component known as an SSH daemon. As a brief reminder, daemons are background processes that are activated and then remain to wait for any commands that may be relevant to them. In this case, the SSH daemon is always on the lookout for a very specific TCP/IP port that informs it of a client connection request.

The client is responsible for starting the connection, and then the daemon will use its own software to directly interact to verify credentials and then allow for the SSH to be established. In order to establish this connection, you will need to ensure that you have the corresponding client and server components installed. A commonly used open source SSH tool is OpenSSH—this will require you to grant access to the terminal on the server and the computer that you are using to allow for the connection to be maintained. If you have chosen Ubuntu, this will not be installed by default, but you may already have it on other distributions of Linux.

You can check quite simply whether you have an SSH client already installed through the following process:

1. Load up an SSH terminal. You can do this by searching for "terminal" or pressing **CTRL + ALT + T** on your keyboard.

2. With the terminal brought up and within it, type in **SSH** and press **ENTER**.

3. If the client is already installed, you will see your access to the other server. If you do not get a response with options and commands listed for you, you will need to install OpenSSH.

Luckily, installing OpenSSH is also relatively simple. You can do so with just a single command:

sudo apt-get install openssh-client

Upon typing in this command, you should be asked for a superuser password. Provide this and press Enter when prompted to complete the installation. You should now have SSH access to any machine that has the server-side application, so long as you have the credentials to prove that you should have those privileges.

Of course, you still need to install the server side component as well in order to truly get access. Again, ensure that there is not already the SSH component installed on the server.

1. From the server machine, open the terminal. Again, you can either search "terminal" or use the **CTRL + ALT + T** command from the keyboard.

2. With the terminal up, type in **ssh localhost**, followed by pressing Enter.

3. Systems without SSH will respond that the connection has been refused.

When the system is refused, you know that you need to install OpenSSH. With the terminal still open, you will want to run the following command:

sudo apt-get install openssh-server ii.

You should again be prompted to enter the superuser password. Then, hit **Enter + Y** to grant the installation permission to continue right after the disk space prompt. It should then automatically install all required files. In order to test that you have been successful, try the following command:

sudo service ssh status

If you have done your job, you should receive a response within the terminal that informs you that it is active and how long it has been running. Congratulations! You have stablished your SSH connection!

Types of Shell

When you are using Linux, you will primarily encounter two types of shells: These are the Bourne shells and the C shells. Each category of shells will involve slightly different command standards, but they will still get the job done of allowing you contact with the shell to interact with and control the computer.

By and large, you will primarily be utilizing the Bourne Again SHell, known as BASH. However, it is never a bad idea to familiarize yourself with the several different options out there for you to utilize for future reference.

Bourne shell (sh)

The Bourne shell is the original shell that had been used with Unix. The prompt that you will see when using the Bourne shell is the $ symbol—this tells you that the terminal is ready for input. There are several other shell types that are recognized as related to the Bourne shell, such as the Korn shell and bash.

- **Korn shell (ksh):** This shell was invented by David Korn in the mid-1980s. It is nearly completely compatible with the Bourne shell, meaning that if you are already using the Bourne shell, you can utilize this particular version immediately. Likewise, a device utilizing the Bourne shell can utilize the Korn shell instead, allowing for versatility. This is a popular shell, thanks to its compatibility with the Bourne shell and the fact that it also offers several desirable features from the C shell while including its own benefits as well. It includes command-line editing, allowing people to change mistakes simply, something the Bourne shell does not offer at all. Along with this, ksh utilizes job control—the ability to stop, start, and suspend commands at the same time.

- **Bourne Again shell (bash):** This is the free distribution of the Bourne shell that comes with Linux systems. It shares a lot of similarities to the Bourne shell that it came from, though some people tend to struggle with it. Luckily, there are several alternative guides that you can use to work through the process of using this.

C shell (csh)

Similarly to how the Bourne shell is deemed the defining shell of a family of others, C shell is deemed to be its own category of shells. It draws its name from the fact that it is programmed in C, and it runs in a text window in which you can insert your commands, which are then read by the program. It boasted features such as interactivity and style, with these making it easier to use, and the language was deemed to be more readily understood by those who were trying to use it.

In particular, C shell had several important features, such as its grammar and syntax, allowing for it to be readily followed, and it allowed for edits to be performed.

Unlike the Bourne shell, the C shell will utilize the percent (%) symbol as the prompt for input.

- **TENEX/TOPS C shell (tcsh):** A derivative of csh, tcsh is entirely compatible with chs. It is more-or-less the csh, though it added in some improvements and enhancements that allowed for more uses for the program. In particular, it allows for command line editing, filename/command completing, and more. Thanks to these features, it is great for those who struggle with traditional Unix commands, or even for those who are slow when it comes to typing. Since the filename will try to complete itself with the press of the Tab key, you are able to type in half of the file name, hit Tab, and have the program try to fill it in for you.

Shell Scripting

Shell scripting, then, is the composition of several commands for the shell to execute. These can combine several repetitive tasks and create one simple script that can remain in storage until it is necessary to utilize, allowing for execution at nearly any point in time. This allows for the reduction of effort required by the end user since the entire series of repetitive tasks can be combined into something shorter. This is perfect if you will be using the same long series of commands routinely. If you combine them all into one script, you can trigger the whole thing to run at the same time, rather than having to write out each command every time you use it.

Remember that shell scripts require a very specific syntax. The shell is comprised of several elements that come together: the keywords, commands, functions, and flow control. Each of these elements plays their own roles and are crucial to understanding in order to truly create the language in a way that the computer can process it. Think about your own language for a moment—word order matters, right? "I can have pizza" and "can I have pizza" have two entirely different meanings—one is confirming permission while the other is asking for permission. Similarly, if you mix up your syntax, your shell will not always be able to understand you.

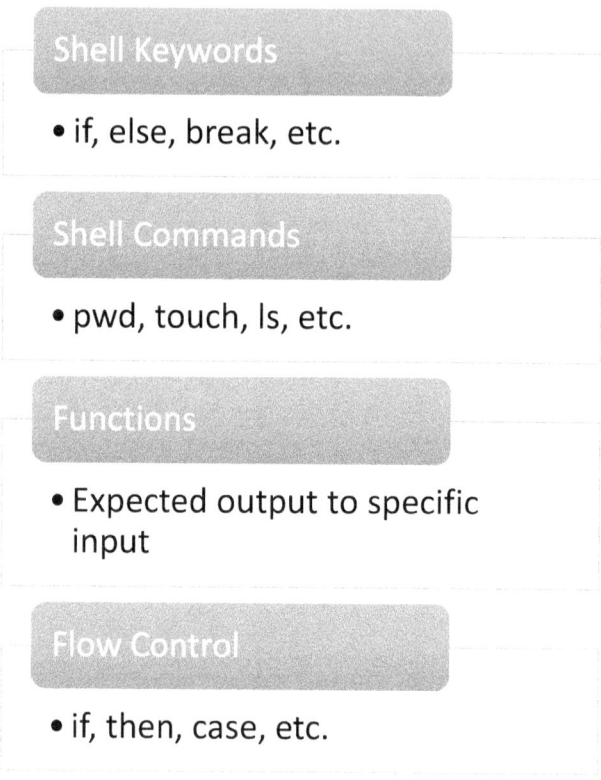

How to shell script

For the purpose of this tutorial, we will be working with bash standards, as that is the standard structure that is commonly used within Linux systems by default.

The steps to creating a Shell Script are not particularly difficult, so long as you are able to follow along. There are five simple steps that you will need to follow in order to create your script. Of course, your scripting is also going to grow more complex as you continue through this book and learn more commands to create more sophisticated scripts in the first place. Consider this a basic guide.

First, you must create your file using a vi editor. You want to make sure that the file is named with **extension .sh** to make sure that it will function.

Now, you must begin the script, utilizing the following code:

#!/bin/sh

The symbol **#!** Is an operator. It is referred to as a shebang, and it directs the script to ensure that it gets to the right shell. When you then direct it to /sh, you are directing it to the Bourne shell.

After you have directed to /sh, you are free to write the code that you want to have executed.

This is where Chapter 5 will come into play—you will learn the commands necessary to create exactly the script that you are looking for or need. When you do finish writing your code, safe the script file in .sh format. Let's say your file is named listfile.sh because you have designed it to list out all of the files present at that point.

When you want to execute your saved script, you will type:

bash listfile.sh

Typing that command will then trigger the script to execute, providing you with the end result. For now, this is all you need to know. As you read through Chapter 5, start to think of some of the potential options for coding the script that you will want.

Basic Command Line Editing

As one final note before wrapping up the chapter on shells, you will be provided a short list for command line editing. This feature can be incredibly helpful to you if you are able to memorize theses commands.

CTRL + L: Clears out the screen

CTRL + W: Deletes the word the cursor is currently on

CTRL + U: Clears out the current command line

Up or Down arrow keys: Recall commands

Tab: Auto-completes file names and directories

CTRL + R: Allows the user to search through the command history

CTRL + C: Cancels the current commands

CTRL + T: Reverses the last two characters before the cursor

ESC + T: Reverses the order of the two words preceding the curser

CTRL + H: Deletes the letter in front of the cursor

Chapter 4 Quiz

Congratulations! You have made it through Chapter 4. At this point, you should have a pretty solid foundation for understanding the Linux shell. Try to answer these questions to ensure you understand the basics before moving on. The answer key will be on the page directly after this quiz.

1. What is a shell?
    a. The kernel
    b. The physical case around the hardware
    c. The program that allows user interaction with the OS
    d. The operating system's type
    e. All of the above
    f. None of the above

2. True or false: Bash is necessary for Linux to run.

3. What does the terminal allow you to do?
    a. Interact with the operating system
    b. Control the computer's functions
    c. Establish ssh connections
    d. All of the above
    e. None of the above

4. Which two shells are compatible with each other?
    a. Bourne shell and C shell
    b. Bourne shell and tcsh
    c. Bourne shell and Korn shell
    d. All of the above
    e. None of the above

5. True or false: The shell is the innermost part of the computer

Chapter 4 Answer Key

1. **C:** The shell is the program that the user will utilize to interact with the system.

2. **False:** It is useful if you wish to have any real control over your computer system, but it is not absolutely necessary. Even if you needed a shell, bash is not the only option out there for you.

3. **D**

4. **C:** Both Bourne and Korn shell users can switch between the two interchangeably.

5. **False:** The shell is the outermost component of the operating system.

Chapter 5: Linux Commands

This chapter is designed to be a sort of accessible dictionary for you, where you can access a wide range of Linux commands on demand in one place. Because, especially at first, you are going to find that you are not quite familiar with the system commands off the top of your head, it can be useful to have a chapter to fall back on to look up the command you will need.

These commands are designed to be used within the terminal, allowing you to directly communicate to the system itself. This means that, through the use of the terminal and the commands provided within this chapter, you will be able to directly influence and interact with the computer. Of course, there are also several rules that you will have to remember when utilizing these commands. Keep in mind first and foremost that $ is prompt to inform you that the individual is officially ready for your input within bash. However, csh will utilize the % to prompt you to enter your input.

Also, remember that the inclusion of a colon after the code within this book is done to separate it from the description of that particular command's function, and the colons should not be included. Beyond that, you must also recognize that Linux is, in fact, case-sensitive. If you enter a code with a capitalized letter that is not intended to be there, it will fail to load up whatever it is that you have prompted it to load in the first place.

This does come with some advantages, such as allowing for identical strings of symbols in the same case to be processed quicker rather than having to process all of the letters to ensure that the letter itself is registered in either case rather than the specific case expected. Even though computers today are more than capable of processing that extra load, a habit has won out, and case-sensitivity remains to be a feature to remember.

System Information Commands

Hardware is incredibly important to be familiar with when you are working with the more intricate matters of a computer. For this reason, Linux comes with several commands that will allow you to access any information about the hardware that you may need. These commands will help you understand the configuration details of several hardware components.

When you use these commands, you will be able to track your current system's ability to function, and this means that you can see how to allocate resources or know how well the system can handle your current tasks. While some distributions will have slightly different commands, these are the most readily available commands out there if you need to gather information about your system.

As you read through these command codes, notice how there are several that seem quite similar, but they all have their own nuances that set them apart somehow.

It can be intimidating to see all of these codes typed out in front of you, but remember, there are tools available to you that will help you if you cannot or do not wish to memorize the commands.

accept: Allows you to accept a job to a destination

arch: Displays the print machine's hardware name

date: Displays the system's date and time

df: This particular command triggers the computer to report the disk space available in the file systems. It reports on several different partitions and their mount points, providing data for all of it.

fdisk: This is the utility command to change partitions on hard drives if necessary to do so.

free: This tells your computer to check the amount of RAM on your computer—free, used, and the total amount of RAM on the system.

hdparm: This tells your computer to provide you with information about hard disk drives or other sata devices.

hwclock: Displays or allows for the configuration of the hardware's clock

hwinfo: This is a general purpose command that probes the hardware—it will provide you with either detailed or brief information about hardware components, providing more than what you may use lshw for.

lnxi: This is a bash script, meaning it contains a larger code. In fact, this particular command has a 10,000 line code within it. In activating this code, you will gather up all sorts of hardware data from several different sources, placing it all into a nice, easy to read a report that even beginners will have little issue navigating.

lsblk: This triggers the device to list out block devices. In doing so, you will see hard drive partitions as well as optical and flash drives.

lscpu: This command will pull up a report about the CPU and processing unit on your computer.

lspci: This command lists out pci buses while also giving you further details about them. It includes the vga adapter, graphics card, USB ports, and more.

With this particular command, you can also filter out the specific information you are looking for thorugh the utilization of **grep**, which will be discussed in further detail later in the chapter.

lsscsi: This command lists out scsi devices, such as hard drives and optical drives.

lshw: This is a general purpose command that will list out all of the hardware installed on your system, as well as the data included within it.

lsusb: This command provides the user with data about the USB controllers and any devices connected to them. You can add in **-v** to your code if you wish for this detailed information to be printed for you.

mount: This is designed to either mount or unmount devices, as well as view mounted file systems currently interacting with the server. Once again, you can utilize **grep** to filter out exactly which files you are interested in seeing.
uname –m: triggers the system to print the machine hardware name

uname -r: triggers the system to print the kernel release being used

System Shutdown, Restart, and Logout Commands

Thankfully, Linux makes it incredibly user-friendly to restart your computer or shut it down. While on most other operating systems, you simply go through the buttons and prompts to select shutdown, restart, or logout, with Linux, you can do this via the terminal as well. For those who are always accessing their terminal, this means that you will be able to manage your system with just a few keystrokes.

Keep in mind that most of these processes will end your current session—for that reason, you must make sure that you are ensuring that you will not lose your work as you go. This section will guide you through the most common shutdown commands. With these commands, you can begin to take control of the system—you can program the system to shut off at a predetermined time or decide to turn off within a few hours or minutes. No matter when you choose as your computer's shutoff time, you will be able to program it in. This is the beauty of Linux—you can program whatever commands you desire within it.

sudo shutdown –h HH:MM: After the –h, you can enter a time that you would like to trigger the computer to turn off. You can enter **now** or in any other time, keeping the format in **HH:MM**, so if you want your computer to turn off at exactly 7:38 PM, you will enter:

sudo shutdown –h: 19:38

Without the time included, you will get a message telling you that you must set a specific time for the shutdown to occur. Instead of using HH:MM or **now,** you can also opt to do **+30** to add 30 minutes to the program.

sudo shutdown –c: this will cancel the currently scheduled shutdown command if you have it set to cancel at a specific point in time. When you use this, you will be able to ensure that you are not interrupted by the scheduled shutdown.

sudo reboot: this will trigger your computer to restart itself.

init Service manager. This will determine the level at which your program is running. There are several different run levels that can be within—from 0-6, s, and m.

- **init 0:** This is shutdown

- **init 1:** This is the single-user mode or emergency mode .There is no network or multitasking.

- **init 2:** There is no network at this stage, but the support for multitasking is available.

- **init 3:** The network and multitasking are present, but there is no GUI.

- **init 4:** Similar to init 3, but used in some research. This state is essentially irrelevant to you right now.

- **init 5:** The network is multitasking, and GUI is present.

- **init 6:** This is used to tell the system to restart.

- **init s:** This tells the system to enter maintenance mode.

- **init m:** This tells the system to enter maintenance mode. Synonymous with init s.

pkill: This will kill a process by name. Killing the processes before shutting off the system is necessary with Linux, or you risk causing issues with the software and files. You can use this to end the sessions of other users as well. When you use this to kill other users, make sure that you do not kill a root user or a system level process or you will kill the server's current processes.

To kill the process of another user, use the following command:

pkill –KILL -u {username}

kill: This will terminate a process.

logout: This will force the logout of a shell. You can also use this if you are a regular user within the computer. It will log you out of the sh or ssh.

Files and Directory Commands

Sometimes, you need to find something within your files and directory. Luckily, rather than having to dig through everything line-by-line, there are several systems commands you can utilize in order to bring it all to the forefront of the terminal for you to access as needed. This list for you is provided in alphabetical order so you can find the commands by spelling as necessary.

cat: This will print the content of a fiile for you. For example, if kitten.txt has a long poem about why kittens are cute and fluffy if you use the following code:

$$\text{\$ cat kitten.txt}$$

you will end up with the long poem about cute and fluffy kittens in your terminal.

cd: This command allows for the changing of the directory to access a new one. For example, if you use the following command:

$$\text{\$ cd /}$$

You will be moved to the root directory. So long as you define the directory that you wish to reach, you should be transferred there.

cd . . This command allows you to move up one directory level. If you are currently looking within a directory named a file, and within that directory, there is another named basket, for example, using this command will move you from file to basket.

cp [file 1] [file 2]: This command allows for the copying of one file into another one. If the name of file 2 is nonexistent on the system, it will simply be copied over. However, if it already exists, the content sharing the same name will be overridden. For example:

$$\text{\$ cp kitten.txt puppy.txt}$$

In this example, so long as there is no other file named puppy.txt, the designated kitten file will be copied and renamed as a puppy.

cp -r [dir1] [dir2]: This will copy the content that is within directory 1 and place it into directory 2. As before, if directory 2 does not exist, it will be created, and if it does exist, it will override the other format.

echo: This will trigger the system to send an input string to standard output. For example, if you are typing input, you can cause the input to be recorded and repeated in the output display.

find: This will allow you to do a search in the file directory for anything you are looking for.

grep: This will allow you to search for input files within a specific pattern and bring back the lines related to the search.

head: This will trigger the system to print the first 10 lines of the file for you to view in the terminal. So, if you use the following code:

$ head kitten.txt

then you would find yourself with the first 10 lines of the kitten poem in the terminal.

less: This command displays the contents of any named file one page at a time.

locate: This can also be used to find a file that you are looking for if you know its name.

ls: This command triggers the terminal to list out the content within the specified directory being used.

ls -la: This command will list out all of the directory's files, including any hidden directories that may be within it.

mdeltree: This is used to delete MS-DOS files, recursively deleting them and their contents.

mkdir: This command creates a new directory if the name you have entered does not exist. For example, if you wish to create a directory, you may type:

$ **mkdir newfile**

So long as you did not already have a directory named "newfile," one would be created for you.

mkdir -p: This adds a bit more customizability to mkdir. With this particular command, you are able to also create subdirectories nested within the one you have named.

For example:

$ **mkdir -p newfile/pictures/puppy**

This would create a directory known as "newfile." Within the newfile, there is a directory formed that is named "pictures." Inside of pictures, there is a directory named "puppy."
more: This allows for the display of content within a file page by page.

mv: This allows for the renaming of files and directories. For example, if you wish to rename kitten.txt into puppy.txt, you would use:

$ **mv kitten.txt puppy.txt**

This particular code can also be used slightly differently in order to trigger the file to be moved from one place to another. For example, let's say we have a directory named file and directory named basket and kitten.txt is currently within the directory named file. However, you want to move kitten.txt to the basket.

$ mv /file/kitten.txt /basket/

This code should facilitate the move, and kitten.txt will now be found in directory basket.

pwd: This command allows you to see exactly which working directory you are in for easy reference.

rm: This causes the deletion of a file that you have dictated. For example, if you wish to delete a text file named kitten, you would use the following code:

$ rm kitten.txt

rmdir: This triggers the system to remove or delete the specified directory, so long as the directory is empty at the time.

rm -f : This command forces the delete of a file, even if the file would otherwise resist it.

rm -r directory: This will delete a directory, its copies, and all of its content.

rm -rf directory: This will forcefully delete a directory, its copies, and all of the content within it.

tail: This command prints the last 10 lines of a file.

For example, if you use the following code:

$ tail kitten.txt

then, you will see the final 10 lines of the fluffy kitten poem.

tail -f: This will provide the last 10 lines of a file, and continue to display the last 10 lines, even as new ones are added. In this instance, if you were writing your kitten poem actively in the file and used the code:

$ tail -f kitten.txt

then, you will find that every new line that you add at the end of the file will display itself in the terminal as the last 10 lines continuously refresh themselves. This is particularly useful if you are using it to check a live activity log so you can constantly see the most recent activity.

touch: This command tells you to create a new file. For example, if you wish to create a text file named kitten, you would use the following code:

$ touch kitten.txt

whereis: This file allows for the binary, source, and man page files for any given command to be located.

Users and Groups Commands

Linux can accommodate multiple users of the operating system, and those users can sometimes be combined into what is known as a group. Effectively, then, the group is nothing but a collection of users that have the same level of access privileges to the OS. Of course, one particular user can be sorted into several of the different groups at the same time in order to grant several different accesses and privileges if necessary.

groups: This command, when provided with a username, will provide you with all of that particular user's groups, and therefore allows you to see his or her access to the system. This is formatted as:

$ groups dad

This would then list out all of the privileges of the user on that system that was named "dad."

When you forego the username, it will display all of the information for the current user that is accessing the terminal.

groupadd: This will allow for the addition of a new group through the format:

$$\text{\$ groupadd mom groupnamehere}$$

With this format, a new group named "mom" has been created.

groupdel: This allows for a specified group to be removed.

groupmod: This allows for specific group definitions and permissions to be edited and modified.

gpasswd: This will allow the admin to alter the group passwords to gain access to the system.

passwd: This allows for the changing of a password for the user activating it.

users: Allows for the current list of active users on the machine to be seen

useradd: This allows for the creation of a new user for the system

userdel: This allows for the removal of a user account and all files associated with it

usermod: This allows for a user account to be modified.

Files Permissions Commands

This section will provide you with all of the information you need in order to change directory permissions. In doing this, you are able to make larger level changes at a group level rather than having to manually change an individual's permissions. When making changes here, you will primarily see three specific letters repeated: r, w, and x. These stand for reading, write, and execute respectively. When you see these added to one of these groups, you can infer that these privileges have been added for a specific file or directory, or if you see them subtracted away from a group, you can infer that they are being revoked.

chgrp: This refers to the ability to change the groups of files and directories. When you use the commands that have the chgrp root, you know that you are messing with the groups of files. In particular, you must keep in mind that all of the groups must have their accounts logged out to assign groups. There are two specific commands for this particular action.

chgrp groupname filename: This will allow you to change the groups of files to a new file.

Chgrp groupname foldername: This allows you to move the groups of files to a specific folder.

chmod: This refers to changing directory permissions.

chmod +rwx filename: this will add permissions to read, write, and execute.

chmod -rxw directoryname: This will revoke permissions to read, write, and execute within that directory.

chmod +x filename: This will allow for executable privileges to the dictated file

chmod –wx filename: This will allow for the permission to write and execute the file to be revoked.

chown: The last of the ownership commands that will be discussed is chown. This will help you change ownership of any given files.
This can allow you to move ownership of a specific folder to another person altogether. Primarily, this is done in two ways.

chown username filename: This will transfer the ownership of the named file to the named user

chown username foldername: This will transfer the ownership of the named folder to the named user.

Archives and Compressed Files Commands

Sometimes, what you need to do with your OS is to create archives or compress files. That is what the following commands are good for—they enable you to be able to take a large number of files and create an archive of them. They may also compress the archive in order to save space, depending on the commands you insert.

gzip: This is used to compress documents into a zip file.

rar: This will create and manage a RAR file in Linux.

tar: This is the GNU version of tar archives. When you use this code, you are able to store several files in a single archive.

unzip: This will tell you whether you can unzip the file, providing you a usage summary of the document. From there, you can choose to extract the file wwith gunzip and then open the file with tar xvf.

unrar: if installed on the system, this will unarchive and unpack the files that they are commanded to.

Chapter 5 Quiz

Congratulations! You have made it to the end of Chapter 5! At this point, you should at least have a general understanding of the several different commands that you can use to control your terminal. Try to answer the next five questions to determine how well you are currently understanding and comprehending the material before moving on.

1. What is the sign that the terminal is ready for your input when using bash?
    a. !
    b. @
    c. $
    d. %

2. What does "x" stand for in permissions?
    a. Exit
    b. Expel
    c. Expedite
    d. Execute
    e. Excel

3. Are uppercase letters acceptable to use?
    a. Yes, the computer reads them all the same.
    b. No, the computer differentiates between the two and will not read an x as the same as X
    c. Sometimes

4. True or false: When you are programming, the order of words and commands does not matter.

5. True or false: If you are looking for a specific file, you will have to search manually.

Chapter 5 Answer Key

1. **C:** bash uses $ to communicate that it is ready to receive input. csh uses %.

2. **D:** x stands for the ability a user or group has to run or execute the program or file.

3. **B:** While computers may be able to differentiate and translate now, the OS is still designed to receive all input via lowercase.

4. **False:** Programming is a language and has a very specific syntax that you must follow. Otherwise, you will start mixing up files and sending things to the wrong place.

5. **False:** There are several commands that are present to help you locate the file you are in need of.

Chapter 6: Control Privileged User

At this point, it is time to begin discussing the security and privileges of users that are able to access your OS or server. Especially today, people seem to think that technology and servers are less safe than ever, but contrary to popular believe, there is actually plenty of support available to keep systems safe and secure. One such way is through controlling privileged users, which this chapter will teach you to do.

In reading this chapter, you will be guided through various types of linux accounts, such as the root user, normal user, and system user. You will discover sudo, which stands for the super user do. This is the command for the system admin—it is the one command that allows access to everything and anything, so long as you are on the right account with the proper privileges to use it. Lastly, you will be walked through the sudoers file. This file is essentially the underlying programming behind the sudo—it controls the sudo and who has access to the sudo command in the first place. All of this will help you juggle the users on your server or machine, allowing you to ensure that the proper security systems are in place. With everything in place and a secure system, you are able to rest easy and feel like your system is truly safe.

Types of Linux Accounts

First, we will be discussing the root, normal, and system users before progressing to anything beyond this. You must have a complete understanding of these three user account types in order to really understand how sudo and sudoers play into the security of the system.

Because Linux is so incredibly flexible, you have the option to create several different types of accounts. In fact, you can have several root accounts if you need them, or accounts with different permissions in different categories. All that matters is that the needs you have are met effectively. Keep in mind that just because you have root accounts does not mean that you should not have some sort of security system in place—you should absolutely have a password protecting the root accounts to ensure that no one else is ever able to access those files and overtake them without your permission at all. This means that you will be able to ensure that the files themselves have yet another layer of protection. Now, without further ado, let's begin to dig into the three primary user types of Linux.

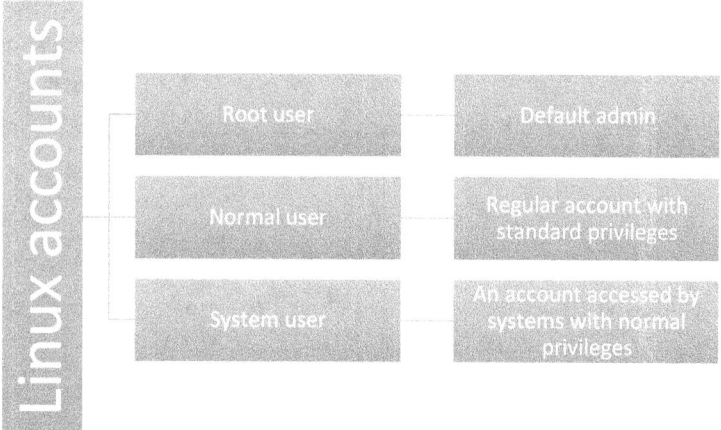

Root user

The first user that you must know is the root user. This is also commonly referred to as the super user, especially in the acronym sudo. The super user or root user is the individual that is on the default admin account. This person has full control over the system, much like how an administrative account would have control over Windows. With the root privileges that are given by default, this user is able to execute any of his or her commands and directly control or alter the services and accounts of other people.

Effectively, this should be your account if you are the one setting up the system. This account is the one that is able to rule over the other accounts, managing and monitoring them all without need for extra permissions. All permissions are granted for the root user. They are able to change the permissions of other users, move files around, change the ownership of files, and do anything else within the system.

Keep in mind that, because you have the power to do literally anything within the program, you will not have the OS telling you not to do something.
There is no safeguard for you, and you *must* be careful when using this account. If you delete a system file, there may be no hope for going back if you have not been regularly keeping archives and backups of your file. If there is a user that is capable of doing catastrophic damage to your program, it is the super user or root user.

Linux assumes that the root user has a pretty good grasp over what they are doing, and because of that, if you are unsure of what you are doing at any point in time, it is better safe than sorry, and you should try reaching out to someone else for help if you think it is necessary. Overall, while this should be your account with your own privileges, you should also try to avoid this account as much as humanly possible in order to ensure that you are not risking destroying everything at all.

There are very specific periods in which you *should* use the root. Otherwise, you are likely going to be fine with just a normal account for most day-to-day functions. Of course, any time that you are attempting a task that requires you to a user the root, you should make sure that you switch over as necessary and back up your data before attempting anything. In particular, you will need to use the root privileges in order to move files or directories in or out of the system directories. Remember, the system directories are those that are directly responsible for the functioning of the operating system, and without them, you cannot run the OS. It is also necessary when you are attempting to copy any of the files into system directories, when altering the user privileges of other users, for some system repairs, and the occasional installation of a program will all require you to use the root account.

Typically, if a file needs root permission to be installed, it is because the file itself will be directly interacting with the system directories. If you are not doing any of the above, just avoid it and save yourself the hassle of potentially messing up.

Normal user

The normal and system users have the same privileges, and both are typically created by the root or another user who has been granted some level of sudo privileges.

The normal user, however, is normally a real person, while the system user is typically a user reserved for software to utilize if necessary.

The normal user will have a real login shell and its own home directory, and each user will also be assigned a UID—a user identification. If this went unspecified during the creation of the new user with the **useradd** command, then the UID is typically automatically selected for you.

Essentially, however, this user does not have any super special admin powers or superuser status. The normal user is able to access any files that have not been otherwise marked as unavailable, and the privileges of the normal fire can be changed regularly depending on what is necessary for the user at any given time.

Most likely, if you are running Linux on your own device, you will have a root account, the administrative account that was used to set up the entire OS, to begin with, and then you will also set yourself up with a normal user account to ensure that you do not accidentally delete something critical or destroy something important. This is your sort of safeguard against an accident. The normal user's own permissions can be customized by the root user—you can grant yourself any permissions that you desire on the normal account from the root account, so long as you know the right way to code it.

System user

The system user, as briefly touched upon, is granted the same initial privileges as the normal user. However, the system user is almost always some sort of software or program, such as a daemon, that will be running in the background and will likely not be particularly interactive. This user classification primarily exists just for organizational purposes. When you are able to dictate the account as a system account, you know at a glance that it is not going to involve any sort of people interacting with it. There may be a daemon running the user, but no person will ever be longed on. While in the real world, this may not necessarily matter technically, it is nice to be able to see at a glance how many human users you have as opposed to daemons running specific software. Usually, these system accounts are created by the operating system during installation, and the OS retains their control. The usually have very specific user ids that you can identify within the root account.

Because these service users will be running processes necessary for the OS, they should be left alone when you are altering, ending, or resetting any processes. You want to make sure you leave these service users alone as much as possible to protect yourself from damaging the software. If you were to damage one of these, it is quite possible that you would destroy the entire OS, which is unfortunately easy to do if you are not paying attention.

Sudo

Now, it is time to discuss sudo. If you are using sudo before a command, you essentially push it up. You tell the system that you are commanding this particular process with elevated privileges that should be respected. Usually, the elevated privileges are what the system checks to ensure that you are actually granted the privilege to make any alterations that you are actually making.

If you have been using Windows primarily, you already have interaction with a sort of example of this account. When you install software, have you noticed how certain installations will trigger a prompt to pop up and ask if you are certain that you wish to proceed and ask for you to give the software the permission it needs to proceed? That is what you are doing in Sudo. You are effectively giving that permission, but instead of with a click of the button, you are telling the system that you have elevated access to the system and should be respected.

If you have been primarily using macOS until now, you have a similar sort of safeguard when you trigger downloads that may be recognized as dangerous or will create major alterations to the OS. On a Mac, you will see a security box pop up, and you must then provide the system with your password to confirm that you do, in fact, want to perform that change on the system. Effectively, then, Sudo is your privilege pass. It is the magic passphrase that tells your system that you are in charge—so long as the privileges on your user account match.

Using Sudo

When you are ready to use Sudo, you do not have to try very hard. Effectively, all you have to do is add **sudo** before the command that you are trying to push forward. If you do this, your program should then ask you for the account password for the account that you are on. If you provide this password and your credentials check out, it will perform the function.

For example, imagine that you want to reboot your system. As you may recall, the command to trigger your system to reboot is simply **reboot**.
However, reboot requires sudo privileges. If you were to simply try commanding your system with just reboot, it would tell you that you must be a superuser in order to execute that particular command.

That is where you would then escalate your command. At that point, you can add to your command, creating an input of:

$$\text{\$ sudo reboot}$$

Your system then asks for the account password, and upon entering the password, it reboots as requested.

Su instead of sudo?

This is perhaps one of the safest ways that you can use to elevate your privilege to trigger the system to obey. There are others, such as the switch user command, known as "su." However, when you use the switch user command, you are asked for the root password and then given the superuser prompt.

You know that you are in the superuser prompt when you get a # as your input ready signal instead of the typical $ that you are likely used to seeing by now. The # should be your warning sign—if you see this waiting for you in the terminal, you know that you are on the root account, and you need to be careful.

While the switch user command may have its uses in very specific situations, it also runs the risk of you destroying everything with a single typo or the act of someone accidentally bumping you while you are clacking away at your keyboard. When you use sudo, however, you are required to insert it for each and every command that requires extra privileges. This means that you have that extra safeguard. Of course, this could get annoying if you were in the process of doing something that would require you to constantly be validating your credentials, but it could be worthwhile if you think that the extra security is worth it. Of course, you could always just set up a backup of your system right before you begin the process of entering your su commands if you wanted to bypass the constant sudo usage, but that is ultimately a personal decision that you have to make, weighing the risk for yourself. Ultimately, the more you are in su, the more likely it is that you are going to have an accident.

The Sudoers File

Underneath sudo is the sudoers file. This determines who gets to use the sudo command in the first place in order to actually make use of the authority it brings with it within the OS. Typically, you can access this file within the location of /etc/sudoers, and you will have to edit this if you want to mess with command values and permissions. Perhaps the best way that you can make user of the sudoers file and the safewst way to editing it is thorugh using the visudo editor.

Visudo

Visudo itself acts as a sort of stopgap—an extra layer of security for the sudoers file. It allows for safe edits while also locking the sudoers file from being edited at the same time by multiple users, which could become dangerous if two people tried to create contrasting edits at the same time. If you try to access the sudoers file with visudo when someone else is currently in it, you will be rejected with an error message and told to try again later.

When you do make an edit, it will stop and check the edits for any errors that may be catastrophic in an attempt to at least try to make sure that you do not completely destroy something important.

Upon finishing your edit of the sudoer file after accessing the visudo editing system, the edit will be scanned for any errors. If you do happen to make a syntax error, it will reject the save, printing the message that declares that there is an error and will tell you which lines that mistake is in. From there, you are prompted to either attempt to re-edit to fix the mistake, or you can quit saving the changes anyway. However, if you quit after visudo has found an error, it is highly likely that sudo will also find the error, and sudo will not be accessible until the error has been corrected.

In order to access visudo, all you have to do is enter the prompt:

$ **visudo**

and you should be granted the access you are looking for, so long as the permissions are right. There are also several other options that you can pair with the visudo function in order to help you really make the most out of the program. These commands include:

visudo -c: This triggers visudo to go into a check-only mode. It will check the current sudoers file for any syntax issues and will print the status of the file. If the check was clear, visudo would end with a final value of **0**. However, if there is any sort of error detected, it will end with a value of **1**.

visudo -f sudoers: This specifies an alteranate location for sudoers, checking or editing the file of your choice instead of storing it in the default /etc/sudoers.

visudo -h: This is the help option, and when you do this, visuo will provide a short printed message.

visudo -q: This tells visudo to enter quiet mode. When in this mode, no details of the syntax errors detected during a search will be printed or pointed out to you.

visudo -s: This will enable the checking of the sudoers file. It will create an error if an alias that has not been defined is being used.

visudo -v: This is the version option—it tells visudo to print out the version number before quitting.

The sudoers file

With the visudo access created, you are then able to begin editing your sudoers file. This is what will provide the sudo access to any accounts. When you first access your sudoers file and scroll to the bottom, you will likely see a line that says something along the lines of:

root ALL=(ALL) ALL

Effectively, this means that the root user can execute from all terminals, like all users, and run all commands. Read all as any for a moment, and you can see how that can be scary. The root user can be basically anything it wants to order anything it wants and do anything it wants. If you want to have any similar powers yourself on other accounts, you will need to set yourself up for an account that is designed as a sudo account.

First, you must log into your server as the root user.

Then, using the command **adduser** you must create a new username.

$ adduser usernamehere

At this point, you will be asked to make a new password for the account. Do not forget your password, and make sure it is actually secure. From there, the command will create a home directory for you. Just press Enter to accept the default unless you feel like filling it in. Then, you must add the new user to the sudo group using the following command

$ usermod -aG sudo usernamehere

This should give you the sudo access, though you should still probably test it. Switch to the new user with the **su** command:

$ su – usernamehere

At this point, you need to test your access. Try using the whoami command to get all of your details:

$ sudo whoami

If done properly, the command will provide the output "root." If it is root, you know that you have access. From here, all you have to do is use the sudo command with space after it before any command you issue. The first time you attempt to use sudo when in a session, you will be asked to enter your password for security reasons. And just like that, your user account will have sudo access, allowing you to avoid any painful mistakes that could cripple your system or ruin your files in any given way. Since you will now have to enter sudo in order to do anything significant or dangerous, you should be pretty secure.

Chapter 6 Quiz

Congratulations! You have finished reading Chapter 6: Control Privileged User. By now, you should have a general idea of how the system hierarchy of users works within Linux and how you can access the right level of security for yourself. At this point, you will be provided with five questions, as usual. Try to answer these questions to determine how well you have comprehended the material presented thus far. As always, the answer key will be provided on the page after this quiz.

1. Which user type has the most privileges?
   a. Normal user
   b. Root user
   c. System user
   d. Random user

2. What is the command necessary to override administrative blocks without having to log into the administrative account?
   a. sudore
   b. visudo
   c. sudo
   d. su

3. Which statement is true?
   a. You should avoid the root user account due to risk of deleting important information
   b. You should avoid the use of visudo editing due to the risk of deleting important information
   c. You should avoid the use of sudo commands due to the risk of deleting important information
   d. You should avoid using Linux due to the risk of deleting important information
   e. All of the above

4. True or false: Visudo will check for errors when you make edits.

5. True or false: Visudo will publish a faulty edit to the sudore file without warning by default.

Chapter 6 Answer Key

1. **B:** The root user has all privileges by default.

2. **C:** sudo is the command used to override administrative blocks

3. **A:** You should avoid using the su root account if at all possible due to it lacking the safeguards of all of the other mentioned processes.

4. **True**

5. **False:** You must command it to save the faulty edit manually, overriding it from warning you about the presence of a syntax error to begin with.

Chapter 7: Basic Network Administration

Thanks to just how flexible and customizable Linux is, it is incredibly versatile in the world of network administration. This makes it particularly useful if you need to run a data center or some sort of server. This chapter will provide you with the last of the information you need to know to get started with your Linux setup. You will be guided through networking as if it were all new to you—because as a beginner reading this book, it may very well be!

Within this chapter, you will learn about the network extension and topology, learning how it works. You will be guided through several protocols, given some information on routing, given some commands that may be useful to you, and you will be on your way. The following chapter will walk you through deciding upon some various software for a Linux distro install, but this is the final chapter with all of the hard, dense material. Congratulations—You are almost to the end!

Networking 101

Networking allows for the connection of computers, phones, peripherals, IoT devices, and more to all connect together, accessing one line of data and being able to communicate. This is the idea with the internet—you are able to access the internet network and communicate with devices that are even on the opposite side of the world from you. There are several important points to consider with networking, but at the base, think of the internet as one giant web—it is all interconnected with several access points for other devices to get to. No matter where you are on that web at that moment, you can get to any other point on the web in some way, even if that way may be slower than it needs to be or should be. This means then that you are able to sort of jump your way around the network to access data that you need, even if it is not on your physical machine. That is how the internet works.

Networking has far more uses than just general web browsing, however. It can be useful for the distribution of data, data storage, general networking, and more. Thanks to this web, we are able to stream videos with ease from anywhere we are able to connect to the internet, or able to access files on the cloud. All that you need is a steady connection, and you are able to access nearly anything that is also connected.

The Network Extension

Networking spreads out across several people, allowing for rapid distribution of data if necessary. Ultimately, the network can be thought of as being divided into three distinct categories: The LAN, MAN, and WAN. As depicted below, you can see that the Lan is the smallest, with the MAN being larger, and the WAN is the largest form of network. Each subsequent network type is going to be comprised of several other aspects of the previous. Essentially, several LANs create a MAN, and several MANs create the WAN.

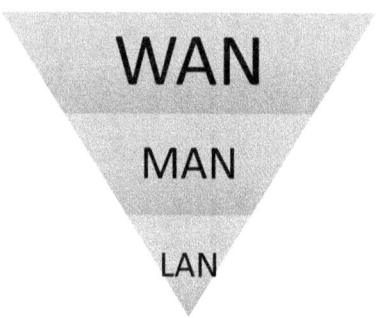

WAN

Standing for Wide Area Network, the WAN is the communication network across any given specified geographical are. It may involve a city or even a country, and these may be public or privatized depending on the usage and whoever is managing it.

To understand what the WAN does, stop and think about the internet—now imagine this as the biggest WAN there is. Several networks are connected together to create one big process. This is what a WAN is—in a WAN, you will have several smaller LANs or MANs that are all within one area, making up the WAN. The WAN is widely connected and is able to reach farther than a LAN. This makes a WAN the best choice if you wish to run a network or a wide-scale sort of server.

LAN

Standing for a Local Area Network, the LAN is much smaller. Usually, the LAN covers a single building, such as a house, or even just a single office in a building. It is meant to be much smaller and not accessed by nearly as many people. They are most frequently connected via Ethernet to control the dataflow, though more and more LANs are moving toward wireless, known as Wireless Local Area Networks or WLANs.

If you have a home setup in which you have two systems sharing access to data, then you have a LAN. Other systems beyond computers can also comprise the LAN, such as printers or smart televisions that will share the data. These are used for the sharing of local data as opposed to wide-scale distribution. However, they are incredibly useful for a home or for a small business.

MAN

Standing for a Metropolitan Area Network, this is larger than a LAN but still smaller than a WAN. This may be, for example, a large tech campus that shares a network spanning several blocks or even several square miles, but is not particularly wide-reaching—this would be a MAN. It can also be used to describe a city. Typically, a MAN is several LANs that create it, and the MAN is a fantastic way to pass forward the data within a LAN, allowing it to stretch further.

The Network Topology

With that understanding of the network itself, it is time to look at the most common topologies—the forms through which networks connect to nodes. The node is an individual device that is connecting to the network in some way, and different topologies will organize these networks in different ways, depending on necessity and what makes the most sense.

Point to point

With this network topology, sometimes referred to as the bus topology, there is a central cable that runs between all devices on a LAN and connects them all. It is easy to connect to, but if there is any sort of break in the system, the whole thing will crash.

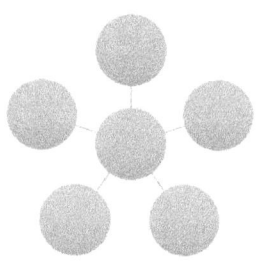

Star

The star topology works to connect several devices all to a central computer that is referred to as the hub, as seen in the picture above. The nodes are able to communicate by first passing through the hub. In this form, a single node's malfunction will not impact the rest of the network, but at the same time, if the hub were to fail, the entire network would be crippled.

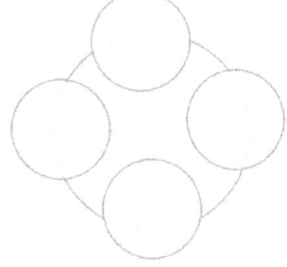

Ring

In the ring topology, a LAN is set up with the topology of a ring. Each node is connected to two others within a closed loop, and all messages will travel around that circle. This allows the message that is being passed along to be regenerated with each node it goes through.

Tree

The tree topology is a hybrid of the bus and star topologies to create what looks like trees when drawn out. It involves several star-configured networks that connect to a single linear backbone. This is great for larger computer networks that are benefitted by being broken into easily managed pieces, but the system is at a disadvantage because the backbone acts as a hub, and if that fails, everything fails.

Mesh

Full mesh topology connects every node to a circuit connecting it to every other node within the network. It is expensive to manage, but it also leads to the most redundancy—which means that it is safer. Even if a single node fails, traffic can continue because all nodes are interconnected. Sometimes, some nodes are organized with a full-mesh pattern while others are not entirely interconnected, allowing for some redundancy and some money saved, while still managing an effective network. This is known as partial mesh topology.

Main Protocols of the Internet

TCP/IP

As a precursor to routing, you must first understand the TCP/IP network model. This is the way that packets are able to find their way back and forth across the internet, allowing them to reach the right host within the network.

Within this network model, there are five layers that describe the necessary processes to actively shift and move the packets from the host to host as necessary, no matter whether that host is local or across the world.

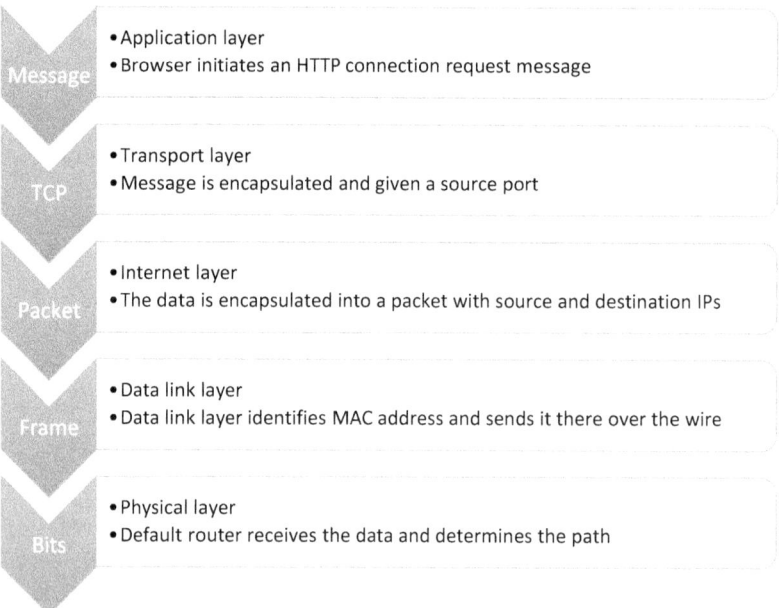

- **Application layer (Message):** It all starts with a message. The first layer consists of the necessary protocols that will be needed for communication, such as HTTP, SSH, IMAP, and any other commands that will be necessary. When you then request a webpage at any point, the message is communicated through one of those formats.

- **Transport layer (TCP):** Next is the TCP segment—this provides the data transport from end to end and also manages the flow. It is independent of the data that is being transported.

- **Internet layer (Packet):** This is done on the internet layer of things. It is the part that routes data across the appropriate networks in order to ensure that they arrive at the proper final destination through the use of IP addresses and routing tables.

- **Data link layer (Frame):** This layer controls and facilitates the direct connections that occur between hardware within a single physical network. It uses MAC (Media Access Control) address within NICs (Network Interface Cards) in order to recognize any devices that are connected to the network. It is only able to interact with other devices and hosts that share a network together.
- **Physical layer (Bits):** This is the layer consisting of NICS and a physical Ethernet cable that allows for the connection between networks. The Ethernet cable is what enables the bits to be transmitted.

IPv4

This refers to the Internet Protocol Address version 4—it is your IP address. With the IPv4, you are using the 4th protocol. Effectively, the IPv4 address will be a 32-bit number displayed in dotted decimal notation. You will see two primary components—the network's prefix and the host number. Every host sharing the same network will also share the same network address. However, each host will also have its own part of the number that is unique.

If the device is accessing the internet and is visible to those outside of the network, it must contain a globally unique number.

TCP

Standing for the transmission control protocol, this is one of the main protocols of the internet protocol suite. It was designed to create a standard that allows everyone to establish and maintain a network conversation because everyone is using data that is compatible. It allows for the exchange of data in the form of packets.

UDP

Referring to the User Datagram Protocol, this is an alternate communications protocol to the TCP model discussed above. The UDP is used to establish low-latency and loss-tolerant connections to allow for high speeds and low risk.

Routing

Now, at this point, you may be considering turning your Linux server into a router—this is a valid point, and several people do it. In order to do this, you must first do a configuration of the router, and then you must assign the address necessary.

Linux as a Router

First, you must configure the device. This will require you to set an IP address on two devices first, making sure that they each use the same gateway IP. Now, what you want to do is set your network to accommodate that gateway IP.

To do this, you must first login to the root account, and then run the command

nmtui

Next, choose the option to **Edit a connection** and hit the **Enter** key.

Choose the available Ethernet that is present on the leftmost side of the window and select **Edit** on the right, once again pressing **Enter**.
At this stage, you will have the opportunity to set your IPv4 configuration to manual. Then, you need to enter the IP addresses that you wish to have access to the network. You can add more if you need to.

Select **Quit** and then press **Enter**. At this point, you should restart the network, and you will need to then confirm that the changes took. In order to do this, you will enter the command:

#ip addr

You should ten be able to see the systems that can access the gateway without accessing the other network. You can confirm this with a ping command. The ping should come back as the destination host unreachable.

Ifconfig command

ifconfig is a CLI designed for network interface configuration. Beyond just that, it also serves to initialize interfaces during boot up. When the server is actively running, ifconfig can further be used to assign IP Addresses to interfaces, as well as enabling or disabling any interaces on demand. This command will also allow you to view the status IP, any hardware and MAC addresses connected, and the maximum transmission unit (MTU) for all active interfaces. Overall, this system command is designed to allow you to debug or to tune the system.

DNS settings

If you find that your DNS settings are misconfigured or you need to change them in some way, there is a simple enough process for this. You will do so by adding name servers to your configuration file.

Within most Linux systems, the DNS will create names defined within the /etc/resolv.conf file. This file will usually contain at least one nameserver line. That line will be the defining line for the DNS server. The name servers will be prioritized by the order that they are found within the system. For ease of access, use the IP addresses of the servers you will be using.

To manage this, you will need to open the resolv.conf file with some sort of editor program, such as nano. In doing so, you will be able to make the changes. If nano is not yet in use on your system, try the following command to install it:

$ sudo nano /etc/resolve.conf

You should then have access to add lines for the name servers you are using. Most often, you will want the one that will be housing any cloud servers you have. With the line renamed, you can then save the file.

Of course, as with after any major change, check the ping to ensure that the domain settings took and confirm that you are, in fact, using the specified IP address.

If you have gotten a message at this point that says that your host was unknown, you may need to try resetting the IP address one more time, as there may be an error within the one that you set up.

/etc/hosts

This command will allow you to configure the DNS locally instead of using external IP addresses. When you use the **/etc/hosts** command, you will ensure that the naming structure is right. It will allow you to manually enter in the IP address and hosts of your choice to confirm that you are able to get the domain name you were looking for.

Diagnostic commands

ping: This is how connectivity is tested. Standing for Packet Internet Groper, ping is regularly used to identify that connectivity between either LAN or WAN. It will make use of ICMP in order to communicate with other nodes on the network.

traceroute: This is a CLI that allows for the tracing of the entire path from a local system to a separate system on another network. It will record the number of hops between router IPs that will have to occur to reach the server necessary.

tracepath: This command allows for the path to be traced to the destination discovering MTU. It will utilize a UDP port.

Similar to traceroute, but this particular form of tracing does not require the same superuser privileges because it has no real options. It is simply informational and will provide all the necessary information .

netstat: This CLI is used to display the information you need to know about your network connections, any routing tables, statistics, and more that will be important to understand with your networking system. It is also used to debug and check to determine which programs are on which ports.

Chapter 7 Quiz

Congratulations! You have finished Chapter 7! You should now have a general idea of how networking on your Linux machine will work and key features that you will encounter. As with previous chapters, it is time for your 5 question quiz. This will help ensure that you understand what has been presented within this chapter.

1. What is a network?
    a. A group of people that you know
    b. A group of devices that are connected together
    c. A group of software that communicates with each other
    d. A group of neighbors that all share the same internet provider

2. What is WAN?
    a. The internet
    b. Wide area network
    c. Widely accessible network
    d. Wonderful access network

3. What happens if the hub of a network goes out?
    a. The whole network stops working
    b. Half of the network stops working
    c. Only the hub stops working
    d. Hubs are obsolete and no longer used

4. Why create a network in the first place?
    a. Easy distribution of files
    b. Sharing data
    c. Connectivity
    d. Redundancy
    e. All of the above
    f. None of the above

5. True or false: You really only need access to a network if you are going to be gaming or otherwise streaming large amounts of data over the internet

Chapter 7 Answer Key

1. **B:** While you do have a personal network, that is the wrong context for this chapter. The network in the sense of Linux is a group of connected devices that are able to share files in some way.

2. **B:** Wide area network. While the internet can be considered a WAN in some sense, it is not what WAN stands for. This is a large geographical area of networks.

3. **A:** The whole thing will stop working. When a hub is implemented, it is the central processing power for the entire network, and without the hub, the rest of the system has no real way to run properly.

4. **E:** All of the above. There are endless reasons that setting up a network could be useful if you have a legitimate need for one in some way. They are absolutely recommended if you need to regularly share files or you want to easily shift from system to system within a home.

5. **False:** In fact, networks can actually work incredibly well as long-term storage for files, which is letting files rest, unused rather than using intensive internet processes that gaming or streaming would involve.

Chapter 8: Alternatives to Windows Applications

If you have made it this far in the book, then you are likely either seriously considering switching to Linux, or you have already decided to do so. Either way, you may have some reservations about the process. For example, it can be somewhat daunting to stare into the face of an operating system that is not designed to have all of your proprietary software. Especially if you have been a long-term user of Windows OS, you are likely going to feel like you do not want to miss out on some of those programs that have been implemented into daily life. After all, you may need access to Microsoft Office in some instances, such as for work, school, or just due to your own personal preference. While running a virtual machine to run Microsoft just long enough to get all of the files you want tis absolutely an option, it is likely not the option that you really want to go with.

Luckily for you, there are several substitutes out there for the mainstream Windows applications, and these substitutes even come with one more bonus—they are oftentimes free. While this may cause you to hesitate at first, wondering if the free software is going to be less reliable or less complete than what you are used to, consider that Linux itself is a free iteration of an OS and you are likely quite close to using that at this point in time. Despite the fact that these projects are free, they are still useful. In particular, this chapter is dedicated to finding you the best popular alternatives to some of the most mainstream Windows applications you will use. From word processing to PDF viewing and all the way to a substitute for digital editing programs, free options that are entirely compatible with Linux exist out there for you.

This chapter will provide you substitutes for the following products:

- Microsoft Office
- Notepad
- Internet Explorer
- Photoshop
- Movie Maker
- Windows Media Center
- Adobe Reader

Of course, the options that are going to be recommended within this chapter are not your only ones—you can go out of your way to locate several other programs and applications that you may find to be more useful to you, and that is okay. Ultimately, using Linux is all about user satisfaction and customizability, so you should absolutely focus on designing it to be functional for you. Feel free to explore your further options to determine if you can find anything else that you would find to be particularly useful for you.

Microsoft Office Substitute

Many people utilize Microsoft Office on a regular basis. In fact, it is regularly used in school settings, with many universities even requiring that their students use this format for the submission of documents. Microsoft Office comes with several different programs within it, allowing for spreadsheets, word documents, and several other forms of documentation to be processed and compiled. If you have been in school recently, you have likely used this at least somewhat. There are, thankfully, several other alternatives to Office, though you may run into instances where you are required to utilize Microsoft Office. Nevertheless, if you can get away with it, you can get by with **Libreoffice.**

Libreoffice is built to be free, and it is admittedly quite powerful. Within this suite, you are given several free and open source office resources. Like Office, it includes several different programs all bundled under one name, each of which produces a different type of document. With LibreOffice, you have access to several different programs:

- **Writer:** LibreOffice's word processor
- **Calc:** LibreOffice's spreadsheet processor
- **Base**: LibreOffice's database processor
- **Impress:** LibreOffice's presentation creator
- **Draw:** LibreOffice's diagram creator
- **Math:** LibreOffice's formula editor

As you can see, all of the major functions of Microsoft Office are provided there with LibreOffice, and for the price tag of free, it almost can't be beat, unless you really *need* to have word doc formatting. While you will be able to open up files created in Microsoft Office in LibreOffice, the converse is not true. LibreOffice is frequently bundled in with many of the more common Linux distros, so you may not even have to go out of your way to locate this particular installation. If you dislike LibreOffice, there are other alternatives as well. In particular, you may find that Open Office or AbiWord is more your style, and that is okay!

MS Notepad Substitute

MS Notepad is usually built in to Windows. It is commonly used as exactly what it sounds like—a notepad. It is a text entry system that you can use to store notes, writing, or anything else that you may have. However, it is far less sophisticated than Microsoft Office. Nevertheless, if you find that you miss MS Notepad, there are substitutes out there for you.

In particular, gedit is the GNOME text editor. It is designed to be simple and easy to use, while also allowing for the highlighting of several programming languages. It also comes with the undo/redo commands, clipboard support, and printing support. Basically, anything that you could possibly need in MS Notepad will be available to you with gedit.

There are also several other types of text editors that you may find to be useful, as well. For example, jEdit, Kate, and NEdit are all other free, Linux-based text editors that may be useful for you.

Internet Explorer Substitute

The vast majority of use on a computer these days is browsing the internet, and if you use Microsoft, you have possibly been using Internet Explorer as your browser. If you are one of those people who ditched Internet Explorer as quickly as you could for something else, there is the chance that whatever it is that you were choosing as your browser is still supported. Internet Explorer itself is not compatible with Linux, but with so many other options available, you are bound to find something that you like.

In particular, Firefox is commonly recommended. Firefox is strongly recommended, even among Windows users, and for a good reason—it is incredibly customizable and offers support for several plugins. It is also actually more secure than Internet Explorer in the first place. Even better, Firefox is compatible with mobile devices as well, so if you prefer, you can set up your system so you are able to access all of your information across your computer and your phone when utilizing this system.

If Firefox is not for you, there are plenty of other browsers available on the market for you as well, and you should be able to find one that works well for you with relative ease. In particular, you may choose to look into Epiphany, Konqueror, or Opera.

Photoshop Substitute

Photoshop is the golden standard when it comes to photo editing software for many people, but unfortunately, it is locked behind quite a large paywall.

Photoshop, while a good program in general, is quite expensive, and also more on the restrictive end. Photoshop is written in C++, making it rather restrictive in general, whereas you do have other options available to you. In particular, you have access to GIMP. Unlike Photoshop, GIMP is written in C and GTK+, making it far more flexible to use. Even better, GIMP is far less strenuous on the processor while still giving you access to several tools. Not only is Photoshop monetarily expensive, it is also expensive on the processor, especially when it is editing files in high resolution.

GIMP typically gets bundled in with most common distros, though you may stumble upon one that does not include it. Nevertheless, try taking a look at it. Even if you do not make the shift over to Linux, you may find that GIMP is a better alternative to Photoshop for you anyway. Beyond GIMP, if you find that it is not quite to your liking, you can try CinePaint as well. These programs, while being recommended for Linux, are also compatible with Windows.

Movie Maker Substitute

Despite common assumptions, Linux actually has several options available for decent video editing programs. While many people may feel like they are missing out if they do not have access to their media editing on Windows or Mac, such as Windows Movie Maker, you are actually able to find alternatives readily available on Linux as well. While Windows Movie Maker is a good option for you, if you have access to it, some of the lesser known Linux iterations are actually more advanced and allow for further functionality that you may not otherwise have access to.

In particular, Cinlerra is designed to be an advanced alternative to Movie Maker. In Cinlerra, you are able to work with ultra-high resolution processing of images. Despite being free, it offers you all of the editing software you could possibly need—and then some. It offers features such as color correcting, motion tracking, mastering audio, and more, all designed to give you everything you could possibly need when shifting over to Linux from Windows.

After all, artistic pursuits should not have to suffer in the name of customizable operating systems. And even better, like all of the other programs that have been discussed in this chapter, it's free. If Cinlerra is not your style, you may find that one of several other options appeals more to you. Other options that you could look into alongside Cinlerra include Kdenlive, LiVES, Open Movie Editor, VideoLAN, and more. All you have to do is dig around a little bit, and you will find several other options for you.

Windows Media Center Substitute

Windows Media Center is the major entertainment system that was released with Windows starting with Windows 7. It allows you to load up videos. However, it was also rather strenuous on the graphics card, requiring a high-end one in order to actually function properly. Because of this, many Windows users ditched Windows Media Player long ago. Even if you were one of the common users of it, you are not losing out on much by transferring over to Linux.

Instead, try taking a look at Linuxmce instead. This program is not just limited to videos either—it can be utilized with several other functions and programs as well, such as security cameras, telecommunication, and also running all of the media that you may have had on your device to begin with. It is meant to be a sort of cohesive program that unites your electrical appliances at home, from lighting to security and media, with everything in between. Since we are discussing this as a media specific replacement, we will focus on the media features. In particular, it is designed to be used to link together several devices on a network, allowing the files that you are accessing to be accessible in several different locations, which further allows you to ensure that you always have your favorite media available. There are also several other options available for a substitute for Windows Media Player, such as Moovida, MythTV, and XBMC Media Center. Try playing around with several of these to find one that really works well for you.

Adobe Acrobat Reader Substitute

Especially in adulthood, Adobe Acrobat Reader is incredibly useful. Necessary to view portable document files (PDF), you must have access to some sort of reader within your operating system. Most commonly, when you use Microsoft, you will end up with Adobe Acrobat Reader. If you do have Adobe Acrobat Reader, you may also be familiar with the myriad of constant updates it puts out, even when little-to-nothing changes. This means that you are constantly being forced to update, even when it is unnecessary.

Of course, if you are leaving behind Windows, you also leave behind this problem. Instead, you can use one of the free and open source software options that will eliminate that problem altogether. Even better, many of these free options are readily distributed with the most common Linux distributions.

If you are going to be running a common distribution, it will likely include either Evince, okular, or Xpdf, all of which are more than capable of meeting your software needs. In fact, Xpdf, in particular, provides you with several different tools that will allow you to do more than just read your files. You will be able to convert PDF to text, PostScript, into PPM/PGM/PBM image files, PNG files, HTML, and more. It can be used to extract metadata or raw images, and will even provide the fonts that were used to create the document for you. It is incredibly versatile, and while it does require you to understand the command line tools, for full optimization, you will find that it is more than capable of getting the job done.

Ultimately, as you can see, there are nearly endless opportunities for all of the major programs you are likely to encounter when using Windows on a regular basis. By just being willing to do the necessary research, you can begin to encounter a far more versatile operating system in general. While it may not necessarily be what you are useful, you do not have to spend an exorbitant amount of money just to get functional software that will do what you need it to. You can, in fact, get that service through the use of plenty of the freeware offered online. As a quick overview, let's recap the most common replacements for the software discussed.

Microsoft Office
- LibreOffice

Notepad
- gedit

Internet Explorer
- Firefox

Photoshop
- GIMP

Movie Maker
- Cinlerra

Windows Media Center
- LinuxMCE

Adobe Reader
- Xpdf

Chapter 8 Quiz

Congratulations! You have made it through Chapter 8. By now, you should have a pretty solid idea of just how much software is readily available to you without having to pay insane amounts of money to access it. Try to answer these questions to ensure you understand the basics before moving on. The answer key will be on the page directly after this quiz.

1. True or false: You can just use your old Microsoft software with Linux.

2. True or false: You cannot use the Linux software on Microsoft

3. True or false: These programs, both the free and open software and the proprietary software, are entirely able to communicate with each other

4. True or false: The Linux software is expensive

5. True or false: You will lose quality by transferring to Linux due to the lack of software available to you.

Chapter 8 Answer Key

1. False

2. False

3. False

4. False

5. False

Conclusion

Well, that brings this book to a close. At this point, you have enough basic information to get started and begin to dabble in the usage of your own Linux distribution that you have chosen, installed, and began to program. Hopefully, you found the process of reading this book informative and useful to you as you made your way through it. The material discussed can be quite dense if you are not technologically inclined, or if you have never really dabbled in tech-related systems before, but it is worthwhile to learn.

The benefits that come from being able to alter and regulate your own operating system, whether from the ground-up if you were brave enough to attempt Gentoo or another advanced program, or even just running an open source distro such as Ubuntu that is designed to be easily accessible, you are giving yourself a whole new world of opportunity. You have the option to directly interact and control your computer. You can influence the processes your computer goes through. You can tell your computer to do essentially anything, so long as you are able to work out the code necessary for it. This coding is the foundation in many much larger projects. What starts as basic coding today can eventually become an AI. What begins as the first attempts at poking around your software can eventually lead to you developing your own OS. Of course, the end result will be what you are willing to put in.

One thing is for sure; however—when you begin to utilize Linux, you are developing a series of skills that are essential to learning.

It can be beneficial to know how to work with computers, and you may even decide to take this from a project to a hobby, and eventually even a career if it is something that has interested you enough to keep exploring. No matter what, however, what is important to remember is that you should make sure you stay up-to-date on your knowledge. From here, you may be ready to install your own iteration of Linux, if you have not done so yet. If this is where you are at in your process, good luck!

It is an exciting time when you are first beginning on this process, and you will surely enjoy it.

If you are unsure whether you are ready to make the plunge into downloading a distribution for yourself, maybe you would find interest in running a few different distros to test first, using the steps listed for you earlier in this book. You can play around with the system, learning which you prefer and which you would rather avoid altogether, which may help you make your decision sooner.

No matter what you decide, however, keep in mind that this was an intro to the subject. This book focused on providing you with the basic essentials to understanding what Linux is and how it works. From here, you may choose to research the specialized distribution you are interested in. You may begin to look into more of the uses that Linux offers and what you can do with the program. You may even decide to continue to books dedicated toward people who are at intermediate or even advanced levels to continue to grow your knowledge. No matter what you choose to do next, if you are willing to put in the time and energy you will find yourself successful in your endeavors. It may not be easy, but the end result will absolutely warrant the end result.

And lastly, if you have found this book to be useful to you in any way, shape, or form, please feel free to leave behind your honest feedback in a review on Amazon. Feedback is always greatly welcome and reviewed!

Kali Linux Hacking

A Complete Step by Step Guide to Learn the Fundamentals of Cyber Security, Hacking, and Penetration Testing. Includes Valuable Basic Networking Concepts.

By: Ethem Mining

Introduction

Have you ever been in a situation where you wanted to try hacking something? Maybe you wanted to test the security of something that you were developing or you simply wanted to challenge yourself, and you were unsure of where to start. If this is something you have considered, Kali Linux may be the OS you need to begin the process.

It is important to note that Kali Linux is not for everyone—you need some level of familiarity with how Linux works or at least an idea of how to interact with Linux if you wish to use Kali Linux in a useful manner. If you do not have this familiarity, it may be in your best interest to go back and begin the study of a simpler distribution of Linux, such as Ubuntu or Mint before beginning to tinker with Kali Linux. If you do decide to move forward with Kali Linux, keep in mind that the tools within this distribution can cause serious damage if misused, and could potentially even lead to significant consequences. This is not a distribution to be taken lightly.

If you decide to proceed, this book will give you the beginner's guide to Kali Linux and how to use it to begin hacking. The first half of the book is dedicated to giving you the basic knowledge that will be needed to truly get the most of the You will be given information about hacking and how it has made cybersecurity more important than ever. You will learn the basics of networking itself, diving into several different concepts and how they work. You will learn all about Kali Linux—what it is, how it is installed, and how to use it, and you will learn several of the most basic Linux commands.

In the second half of this book, you will begin to discuss the utilization of Kali Linux for several different purposes. You will learn about Nmap and how it can be used to detect and exploit vulnerabilities. You will be guided through the steps of remaining anonymous. You will dive into Metasploit and how to make use of it with Kali Linux. You will learn about digital certificates and how to use them, and finally, you will learn about bash (Bourne Again SHell) and Python scripting and why the two of them are sometimes considered to be at odds despite the fact that they could very well work together and cooperate to get much better results than if they continue to be left separately.

By the time you have finished reading this book, you will have an idea of the foundational information you will need to first decide whether Kali Linux is for you, and if it is, you will know how to get started with it and have an understanding of just how powerful this distribution of Linux is. While Kali Linux is not for everyone, if you do happen to fall into the category of people that would find use in this program, then the tools that will be provided with this distribution are incredibly valuable assets that you will not want to miss out on having in your arsenal.

At the end of the day, you will be able to determine if you are happy with the idea of Kali Linux and whether this is for you or if instead, you should be making it a point to move on to a different distribution of Linux instead. You will be able to decide if you want to continue to work entirely with the shell or if you want to learn Python instead. And, if none of this that has been discussed makes any sense, then by reaching the end of the book, you should find some clarity with the topics at hand and how they should be used.

Part I

Introduction to Kali Linux and Hacking

Chapter 9: Introduction to Hacking

It is one of the worst things that could happen to many people—they log into their bank account or credit card only to realize that their account balance is completely drained or that someone has been making heavy use of their credit card. This can absolutely devastate many people, and unfortunately, these days, this is a very real concern.

These days, financial information is backed up somewhere. Your bank has a record of your account number, your card numbers, and everything else someone would need to access it. You likely log in somewhere to pay credit card or utility bills. You may even do the bulk of your shopping, both for groceries and other times online. This means that your personal information is constantly being used online. You enter your social security number to apply for a credit card.

The three major credit bureaus keep your information, tracking and regularly updating it. You may even apply for taxes online. This has one serious implication—all of your essential information is available online somewhere. To be fair, this information is usually stored behind all sorts of safety protocols that are put into place. They are meant to protect your information from being leaked to people who may be interested in using your information for nefarious purposes, but just like armor, there is usually some way to get through it. Some systems may be safer than others but at the end of the day, a dedicated individual would be able to find some way to break through if they put in the effort. As soon as they break through that security system, they have access to any and all of that data, which can then be released and sold, ultimately leading to you having your identity stolen. Everyone wants to avoid that unfortunate outcome, but with the storage of valuable information comes the risk of attack and exploitation, which must be accounted for.

What is Hacking?

Hacking, then, is the act of identifying any sort of weaknesses within a computer or network's security system and then exploiting that weakness in order to gain the necessary access to whatever is hidden behind the firewall. For example, a common example is the usage of an algorithm designed to identify a password in order to sort of digitally pick the lock of a network or account. That account has then been exploited to get the desired access.

Hacking may not always be done with the intention to harm—some people do so for legitimate means, such as to locate a flaw in the system to repair it. Others may choose to do so in order to entertain themselves, not unlike doing a complicated puzzle or trying to solve increasingly complicated math problems to test and hone abilities. Others still do so in order to steal information for some purpose, whether to use it for financial gain or to cripple the system that they are hacking.

Hacking can come in several forms, such as tricking someone into clicking on an attachment in an email that will grant access to a computer. Other forms, however, require far more technical knowhow, developing the ability to trick and trigger the system to grant access and information that should otherwise be safeguarded. This book will primarily discuss methods related to technical expertise rather than using backhanded attempts to fool someone into granting access in the first place. Essentially, hacking is the act of getting into someone else's system, but the methods of hacking can vary greatly.

Each of these occurs in different manners and serve different purposes, but the end result is the same—they allow for information to be stolen and used, or for programs to be used in ways that they were unintended to be. For example, some people may hack their video game console to run emulators to allow them to play ROMs of different games, including some that may not have been intended to be used on that system in the first place. Others may use their skills to steal information and sell it to people looking to steal an identity. Nevertheless, there are numerous options for a hacker to use in order to gain access to all of the information they desire. The rest of this section will discuss some of the most common hacking methods that are out there, allowing you to get a glimpse into what hacking can entail. Keep in mind that this list is not exhaustive.

Malware

Malware is malicious software—shortened down into one word. It includes software such as viruses that are installed, either by you clicking on something that allows it to be downloaded or downloading it yourself, but once you allow it in, you have compromised your information. Attackers will generally use a link or an email attachment that appears to be harmless in order to trick you into installing whatever malware was hidden within. The installed malware can cause all sorts of issues, such as monitoring the usage of the computer, such as keystrokes, which then allows the hacker access to all sorts of information that may be personal or sensitive. It can also grant full access to the computer, depending on the malware that was installed. Overall, however, the vast majority of the time, the user of the computer will have to do something that triggers the download of the malware.

Session Hijacking

As will be discussed later, when a user is browsing the internet, the user's computer sends several transactions to the website's servers, allowing the website to see who is accessing it, what is being requested, and sending the proper information back to the user to display. This is done via routers and networking, and when done properly, you are able to access the information requested without issue, whether you are simply browsing through sites and clicking on links or whether you are entering in sensitive information. This data is supposed to stay private, given a specific session ID that allows the server to know who is using it and how it is able to send the specifically requested data back to the individual asking for it. However, sometimes, that data gets intercepted. Essentially, what happens is that someone else is able to access that unique ID. They are able to use that same ID and make requests as you during your interaction, allowing the attacker to see any of the sensitive information. Sometimes, instead of just observing and intercepting information, the attacker can act as either the website or as the individual using the website, allowing the attacker to request and intercept information from either direction. When this happens, it is known as a man in the middle attack.

SQL Injection

SQL (usually pronounced "sequel") is an acronym for the structured query language. It is the programming language that is primarily used as a means of communication with databases. When a website or a company needs to store sensitive and critical information, such as patient or financial information, the server that it is stored in will most commonly utilize SQL to manage it.

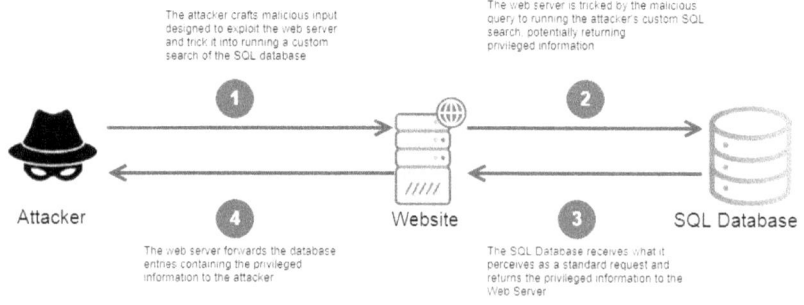

The SQL injection, then, seeks to use code designed to trigger the server to provide information that is normally protected. Especially when the server is holding important personal information, it can be a valuable target—that information can either be sold off or used as leverage to blackmail. Effectively, the SQL injection attack exploits one of the known SQL vulnerabilities, which the attacker takes advantage of. This could be done by inserting a specific code into a search bar or otherwise engaging with it in a way that triggers unintended results.

Phishing

For those who know better than to open up a random attachment or link that has been sent to them, there are other methods to use to trigger you to click. The attacker may know that you are not likely to simply open up a random attachment, so they make the reason to open said attachment one that is compelling and motivating. These people will often imitate other people in order to make you click on the link. For example, you may receive an email from someone claiming to work for the IRS and saying that you have an outstanding balance with them. They do not specify the balance, but they include a statement attached to the email that you are required to click to see it. Of course, the entire situation is fake. There is no balance owed, and if you were smart, you would remember all of the warnings that go out every year about how the IRS will only contact you via snail mail. Phishers rely on you not knowing what you are doing, getting too curious, or not being cautious enough to go through the process of double-checking sources before downloading a document.

DOS

Have you ever tried to leave a big event from a small town? Especially if there is only one road that accommodates leaving, you may get stuck in traffic for hours. The same kind of occurrence can happen with websites—usually, the servers are only able to accommodate so much traffic, and if traffic gets too bad, the website is overloaded and cannot load the necessary sites for anyone.

Sometimes this happens legitimately, such as if highly desired tickets go on sale at a specific time that is anticipated to sell out, or during massive, limited quantity sales.

However, sometimes, an individual may decide that they want to see that sort of full stop happen. When they do so, they intentionally flood the website with traffic—so much that the site's servers can no longer accommodate the load, and no one is able to access anything. Known as DOS (Denial of Service), this attack usually comes from a single source all at once.

However, sometimes, it comes from several IP addresses at the same time, using different computers to attack and making it harder to track and stop. This is known as a DDOS—Distributed Denial of Service.

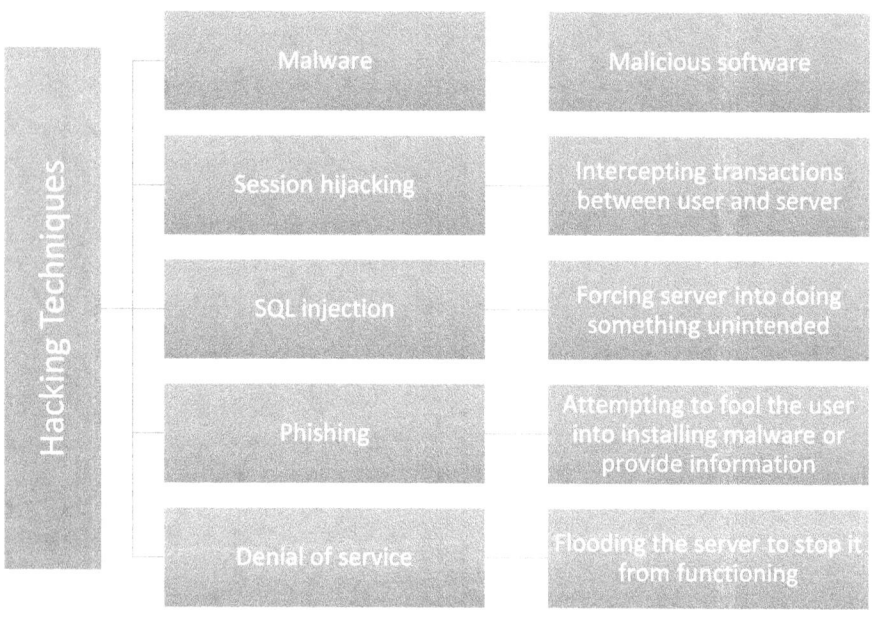

Reasons for Hacking

Ultimately, the reasons for hacking can vary greatly from person to person. Some people do it to learn more information. Others do it to cause harm. Others still do it for entertainment or just to learn how. It has become trendy in modern pop culture to discuss the hacker as a major threat to the internet and cybersecurity. This can make for a particularly convincing villain in a story or film, but real hackers are just as capable of wreaking havoc. On the other hand, there have been politically or socially motivated hackers who use hacking to get attention toward a specific event or to bring forth sensitive information—these people are known as hacktivists.

No matter the reason for hacking, one thing is for sure—unless the hacking is done in order to help prepare the system that is being hacked in order to better the security, hacking is dangerous. It is harmful. It is not a toy. It is not something to be taken lightly. If you are in this book because you want to hack someone or exact your own revenge on someone because of something that has happened or you simply want to watch the world burn, stop. Close this book. Go find a hobby doing something that is not going to potentially ruin lives. Ultimately, lives *have* been ruined by hackers before. Hackers have been able to destroy people, their livelihoods, their careers, and sometimes even their families. Through the stealing of identity or funds, or through causing a disruption so large that a company has gone over or with any other negative implications, hacking can hurt people, and it should not be treated lightly. This is exactly why cybersecurity is such a rapidly growing field.

Typically, people will have one of four reasons to maliciously hack a server or computer:

- They seek to gain financially, such as through stealing credit card numbers
- They build up their reputation within the hacker community through hacking and leaving some sort of identifiable mark on it
- They are engaging in corporate espionage—the attempt to get a hold of a competitor's sensitive information to get the upper hand in the marketplace
- They are entering a government-sponsored hacking attempt to get national intelligence, weaken infrastructure, or just to wreak havoc.

These people do not care about the rules or laws, and in fact, have created a need for cybersecurity and cybersecurity laws, which will be discussed later within this chapter. People hacking into databases and servers has led to a need to make sure that these are more secure than ever, leading to the creation of the entire field of cybersecurity jobs. Hackers are usually classified with titles referring to hat colors. They may be black or with, red or green, or even blue. Understanding these hat colors can help you get a better grasp on why people may choose to hack, more specifically than the four reasons listed above. It may also help you clarify why you have a desire to learn to hack via Kali Linux yourself.

Black Hats

When you think of a hacker, it is most likely a black hat—they do so for nefarious reasons. These are the ones who are often found breaching servers and exploiting weaknesses. They do so to steal and make money. These people, though criminal, are also making use of some of the most basic techniques that are learned. Though they are quite intelligent, they are motivated by less-than-honorable means—all they care about is what they stand to gain.

Grey Hats

Grey hat hackers are a little more complicated than black hats. They are hacking to steal, but usually on less nefarious terms. They may be interested in sharing files or breaking into software in order to use it without paying licensing fees.

They are usually interacting with servers and networks in ways that are exploitative, but not necessarily to steal the information within it. Instead, they treat their hacking more like a hobby that they enjoy. They typically will not inform sites when they have found exploits, but they are likely to offer to fix it for a fee. Essentially, these people are more motivated by seeing themselves and proving to others that they are important.

Red Hats

If we were discussing the personality alignment chart right now, red hats would be the equivalent of the chaotic good player—they are interested in stopping black hat hackers, but they do not want to feel like they are constrained by rules and laws. Instead, they will intentionally subvert any authority and go about their attempts by their own rules. If using the expression fighting fire with fire, the red hats will fight a torch with a flamethrower— they aggressively attempt to destroy the black hat's access to the networks upon figuring out who the black hat is, with the intent to render the black hat completely incapable of doing any more harm. Though these people tend to exist further out from the rest of the hacking community, they tend to be some of the most sophisticated, wanting to play by their own rules.

Green Hats

In the hacking community, green hats tare the beginners. They are usually attempting to learn how to hack in the first place, and will readily ask for help or seek out new knowledge. They are motivated by their desire to learn and develop their skills, ambitiously following their dreams without necessarily having any clear path that they want to follow. However, because they lack life experience and technical knowledge, they also stand to be some of the most dangerous because they have not yet learned just how dangerous their actions can be, nor do they know enough to reverse any damage that they have done.

Blue Hats

Blue hats care about revenge. Though they can be malicious, normally, they only channel their attempts to hack toward whomever they feel has wronged them. Usually, they are relatively new to hacking in general, possibly even script kiddies, but when something bad happens, they may decide to put their newfound skills to good use and set out to intentionally and maliciously hack a target. They do not want to better their skills—they only want to have the technical skills to cause problems.

Script Kiddies

These people do not get a color, but they are still important to mention. These people are usually uninterested in stealing information, but they still find enjoyment in taking codes that are already created and injecting them into servers in an attempt to cause problems. They are most likely to utilize their skills in techniques such as a DDoS to flood a website just to annoy people without any real purpose.

Hacktivists

As briefly touched upon, hacktivists are those motivated by politics. They may be lumped into the black hats, though they are usually hacking in an attempt to bring to light something of importance toward their cause. They may try to release information or records that are supposed to be kept under wraps, or they may decide to actually cause issues for a company. They may even attempt to fight terrorist groups thanks to their impressive working knowledge.

They are trying to lead to positive change, even though they may be using negative methods to achieve it. They are motivated by their cause above all.

White Hat (Ethical Hacking)

The last classification of hackers is the white hat—these are known as ethical hackers. The ethical white hat hackers typically are hacking in an attempt to bolster defenses. These people are intentionally trying to hack into the software in order to help a company strengthen its own defenses as exploits and vulnerabilities are identified. These people are most often found in cybersecurity careers, trying to help keep your sensitive information safe and secure from other people's attempts to steal it. These people are often trained in IT security or computer science and then certified by the EC-Council. This means that they must complete an intensive class and pass an exam, which often involves the training on how to handle the most common and current security domains with hundreds of attack techniques and technologies. The white hat hacker must also maintain these credentials with annual education credits.

Typically, if you want to become a white hat hacker, you are interested in helping people. You want to defend people and you want to do it in a way that is lawful, acceptable, and beneficial to everyone involved. You want to eliminate the vulnerabilities within the system to protect it from damage rather than attempting to go vigilante justice on someone such as the red hat hackers, who may have their hearts in the right place but go about things in a way that is just as bad and destructive as the black hat hackers.

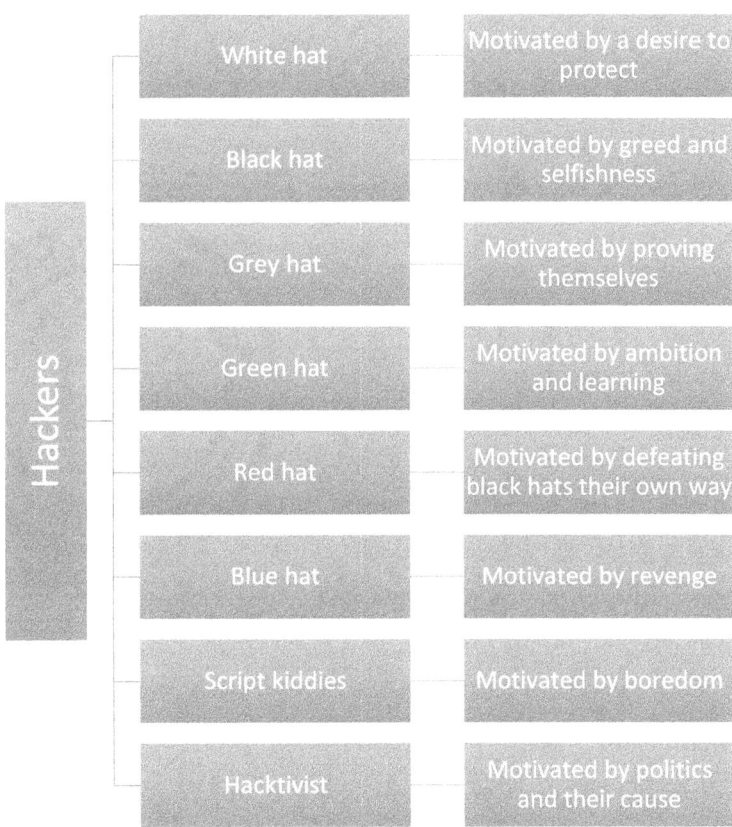

What is Cybersecurity?

As touched upon earlier, the invention of servers and the birth of hackers also brought with it the creation of cybersecurity. Cybersecurity is crucial for those who are intending to rely on servers and databases—without cybersecurity, there would be no defense system. Cybersecurity allows for the defense of any internet-connected system, meaning it protects your hardware, software, and data from falling victim to cyberattacks.

When what needs to be protected is on a server or a database of any sort, there are two different ways that it must be protected—physically from being damaged or taken away, and also digitally in order to protect from those who attempt to access it via the network and steal or harm protected information. Cybersecurity, then, has one specific goal: protecting IT assets from being attacked in order to ensure that the information and data that is housed within those IT assets remain protected and secure for the benefit of everyone.

Because so much data out there is so quite sensitive and should be protected, cybersecurity is absolutely essential. Not only the individual user's data is protected when implementing cybersecurity practices, but the company implementing the practices is also protecting itself. Because the likelihood of a massive breach drops with the usage of cybersecurity, the likelihood of major negative press attention also goes down. Cybersecurity helps lessen the risk of breaches, ransomware attacks, and identity theft of individuals, and though cybersecurity can be difficult to maintain due to the ever-changing world of technology and IT, maintaining it has serious benefits.

Cybersecurity practices should be used by anyone who is using anything connected to the internet—whether you are an employee, an owner of a server, or an individual user, there are steps that you can take to avoid falling for the traps of hackers or those who seek to exploit your data. It all begins with your password.

However, there are also many other points where the security of your personal data as a user is no longer in your own hands and it is up to the company in charge of your data to protect it. Unfortunately, cybersecurity runs into one specific problem that is not likely to go away any time soon: Because technology is constantly evolving and changing, and because networks and data standards change as well, as do hackers, who inevitably find more exploits, cybersecurity is an endless job. There will always be another exploit to find and patch up. There will always be another attempt to steal data. This means that the cybersecurity profession is not likely to go anywhere any time soon. Typically, these threats are approached by focusing the bulk of the resources on protecting the most crucial components to protect against any threats that are known to be out there and significant. However, this approach also leaves some systems either less defended or undefended or leaving the system open to threats that may be deemed to be less known, or those that are less dangerous.

The Elements of Cybersecurity

Cybersecurity, despite the constant fluctuation and change in the system, also has a series of elements that must be maintained. These elements are essentially the backbone for cybersecurity—it needs to have each of these to be deemed successful and truly protect the data and infrastructure it was tasked with. These elements include:

- **Application security:** This lessens the likelihood that any sort of unauthorized code will be able to find a vulnerability

- **Business continuity planning:** This helps maintain or resume any critical functions if something catastrophic happens

- **End-user education:** Teaches the employees or users how to act in order to protect the information

- **Information security:** Protects information

- **Network security:** Identifies, prevents, and reacts to any threats with security policies, tools, and IT.

- **Operational security:** Classifies information and protects it

Information Security: The CIA Triad

As noted just prior, one of the elements of cybersecurity is information security. This particular element is so important that it warrants discussing in its own section. Within information security, there is a concept known as the CIA triad. This particular triad stands for confidentiality, integrity, and availability, which serve as the mission statement of sorts for the information security side of cybersecurity.

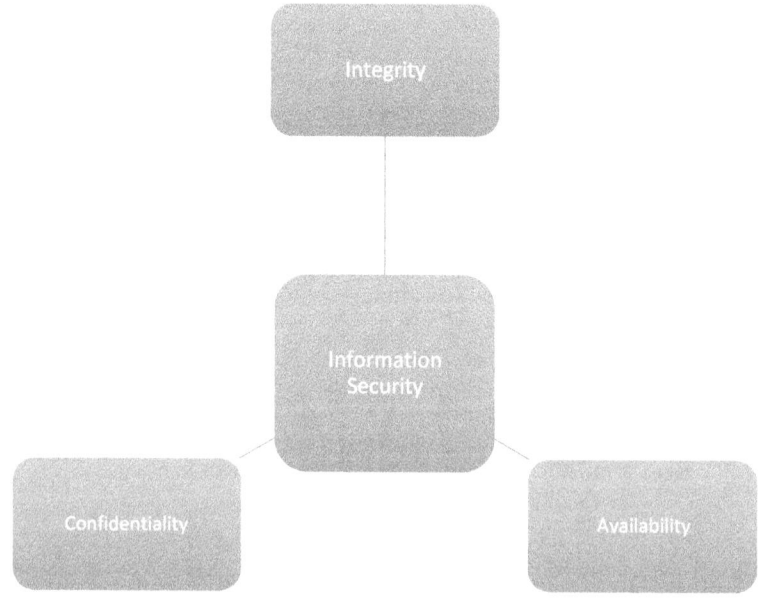

Each of these three sides to the triad is crucial: Information protected must be confidential, accessible, and maintained with integrity. Without achieving all three of these goals, information security has not entirely been achieved. These are the fundamentals for information security, and will always be the core objective.

Confidentiality

This is the ability to protect information from any sort of unauthorized access to it. When information is confidential, it is not accessible by anyone that is unauthorized. For example, when you go to the doctor's office, your medical history is confidential unless you sign a release form. In the medical setting, that information is protected by both security measures as well as regulations for conduct to protect your sensitive medical information from becoming well-known. In the information security side, the information that is being protected will only be accessible by authorized users, with unauthorized users automatically being rejected upon failing to provide the right credentials. For example, consider a credit bureau that has access to all of your personal information, from your social security number to the accounts and account numbers of any of your credit lines—if their data is not secure, you are at risk of identity theft.

Integrity

Integrity is achieved when information is held in a way that is accurate and consistent. This means that its intended and original structures are maintained without any prior authorized changes to the material in the first place. While it is possible that information gets changed if the user is careless or used or if there is an error, however, integrity will be maintained so long as the information is unmodified during storage, being transferred to the requester, and when being used, short of anyone actively and consciously changing it. This means that the data is accurate and kept constant. For example, imagine that you have checked your bank account before going to buy a new computer because you wanted to make sure that your direct deposit check had, in fact, been deposited. If your banking app does not update properly or reflect the fact that you did, in fact, get paid, you are going to think that you are unable to buy that laptop or any other need you may have had.

Availability

The final goal, availability, refer to the information being readily available whenever and wherever it is requested and needed. Because information is generally protected, it is not available to everyone, but it must be available to those with the proper credentials. This should be maintained as much as possible—data protection without ready access to it is not exactly the most useful in situations where data becomes essential. For example, imagine that your medical records are being protected. If your doctor were unable to access your medical records on-demand, you would not be able to get the proper treatment.

Chapter 10: Introduction to Networking

With the wide-scale use of the internet comes the introduction of networking. While it may be easy to think that the information or requests that you put through the internet simply appear instantly after being beamed up to a satellite, especially if you are using a router for a wireless home connection, what actually happens is that the data that you push through goes through wires to get the information you have requested to be returned to you, all at lightning-quick speeds. This is the creation of the network, and whether you have ever considered it or not, it is a massive part of everything in this day and age, and you most likely use the network several times a day. Whether you check your bank account or even buy something with a debit or credit card, you are sending information through a network.

What is a Network?

Defined simply, a network is two or more computers that are connected together in some way in order to share information or interact in some way. The computers do not have to be connected via wire—they can be connected through infrared beams, through the transmission of radio waves or satellites, or even through wires. However, they are always connected in some sort of way.

There are several instances in which a network is a right choice for the usage that is planned out. For example, imagine that you have two computers (a laptop and a desktop), a tablet, and a cell phone.

You regularly use all four items at home and want to make sure that data that is attached to your laptop, which you use primarily for being able to access and browse the internet or answer emails, is also available on your more powerful desktop, which may be reserved for more intensive programs, such as playing video games or editing large files or videos. You also, just for convenience, would like to make sure that your photos that you take on the go with your phone are accessible from your other sources as well. When you want that level of connectivity, where you are able to access all of your files from anywhere, you are looking for a network connection. In getting that network connection, you are able to share those files with ease.

Of course, there are other ways that networks become crucial as well. If you work for a school, for example, you may be familiar with computer labs. In these labs, students put in their login information from any computer to pull up the same account. Teachers can also submit their information to log on from any computer on that network as well, so long as they use the right password and username.

Types of Networks

Networks themselves can come in several different forms. These networks are used for everything and anything that involves the transmission of information, whether you are printing a document or sending an email. It is important to understand that, when discussing networks, you are primarily discussing one of two different network types, though there are several others, depending on the purpose. The two that are most commonly discussed are LAN and WAN, with VPN being a close third. These three types of networks have their own specific usage scenarios. This section will give you a brief overview of LAN, WAN, and VPN, though you will find that VPN gets discussed in more depth in later chapters.

LAN

The most common of the networks in modern-day understanding is the LAN. This network type is known as the Local Area Network—it connects computers and low-voltage devices to one another within a small or local area. This may be within a single building or even a couple of buildings that may need to share information. With the use of a router, a LAN can interact with a WAN in order to transfer data quickly and securely. If you are going to be setting up a personal network at home, it will most likely be a LAN, especially if more than one person shares it.

WAN

Standing for a wide area network, WAN allows for computers to connect from further distances apart. This means that computers, even far from each other, are able to be connected to each other through one means or another. This can be on a smaller scale, such as an internet service provider that is connected to several different LANs, stringing them together into one cohesive network together. Another more well-known type of WAN is the internet. The internet allows for the connection of computers across the world.

VPN

VPN stands for a virtual private network. It is a network that has been extended across the internet as if they were accessing a private network that others cannot access, though the internet. These can also be achieved remotely, through the use of a virtual point-to-point connection, in which the private and remote sites are able to access each other. They are routed through the internet from a private network in order to transfer sensitive information and ensure that it is secure. Typically, it was done by encrypting the data—making it so it cannot be read easily by someone who is not supposed to have access to it in the first place.

Network Address

A network address is a way that the nodes and hosts within a network are able to be identified. Just as your house has an address that allows for snail mail to be delivered exactly to your address, wherever it is, your computer has its own sort of address.

By addressing something to your specific address, someone even on the opposite side of the world will be able to send you something. The network works much like that—it allows you to send something to a very specific point, even if you are not connected physically in any way at all.

In fact, you can even send it across the ocean from one continent to another with ease, so long as you are able to send the request to the right place.

In order to really begin to understand network addresses and how they are relevant to hacking, Kali Linux, and understanding computing in general, you must first understand some important concepts. This section will guide you through understanding and defining nodes, hosts, IP addresses, both public and private.

Nodes

Nodes are the individual redistribution point within a network's connection— if you were sending something via snail mail, the nodes would be all of the individual post offices through which the mail passes. If you send something from Alabama to a remote town in Alaska, that one letter is not going to directly travel to that remote town—it is going to pass through several checkpoints that act as redistribution points. The node may also refer to the final endpoint as well.

It is effectively every location to which the data has been forwarded until eventually it reaches the end of the line and is delivered to where it was supposed to be.

Hosts

The host is a computer that is connected to another computer that is responsible for sending data. The host is a network node—it receives and sends information and has its own address. This can be a server that is holding information as an archive, allowing other people to access it. It could also be a person to person host, in which you have one computer that is holding all of the information in which you are going to access from another. In the sense that a host of a party is the one providing the fun, food, and festivity, the computer host is providing all of the information that is desired. In order to be deemed a host, the computer or server must have its own network address.

IP Address

IP addresses are your "Internet Protocol" addresses. This is the unique address assigned to your computer's online activity. Continuing upon the post office model of the network, think of your IP address as the return address in the corner of the envelope—it allows for the network and the website or server that you are accessing to know that it is your particular computer accessing it, and allowing the server to send the proper information as requested back to you. Without this address being nicely provided for you, the information that you have requested is not as likely to make its way back to you, despite needing to. These IP addresses are not static based on the computer; rather, they are provided by the internet service provider (ISP) for you. Since the ISP acts as your gateway from your LAN to the internet, it also tags your requests with the IP address assigned to your home or access point.

It allows the computer to make that connection to the internet and then granting you access to it. It is able to connect further through the use of internet protocols, which will be discussed later within this chapter. This means that any time you connect to a new internet location, even from the same computer, you will be given a new IP address. The local wifi at the café will give you a different IP address than the one you have at home or at work, even if all three were accessed from the same computer. This is because, when you are on a new internet location, you are accessing the internet from a new location. Your information needs to take an entirely different route to reach you based on your location.

Public vs. Private IP address

IP addresses primarily come in two forms—public and private. Each of these is assigned in a slightly different way in order to allow for the necessary access to where they are supposed to go. The public IP address is the one discussed earlier—it is the one that is designed to allow access to the internet that is provided by the ISP. It is globally unique and can be discovered quite easily, either through commands in the terminal when using Linux systems or through the internet. Just searching "What is my IP address" online should provide your public IP address to you.

A private IP address acts similarly—it provides a computer a specific address, but in this case, it is used on computers within a private space or network without ever exposing that particular device. Think about a LAN—you may have several computers all on the same network. In this instance, the individual computers all hooked to your private network have private IP addresses.

These IP addresses are not tied to the internet, but the connection point, likely a router, is able to send information to the right private IP address. The router, then, gets the public ID while the computers connected to the router get private ones.

Assigning an IP address

There is also a third type of IP address—the static IP address. This IP address will allow you to use various network services without needing to have the IP address of the system that is hosting the services. This can be done in several ways, such as binding the MAC address to an IP address or in setting one up in a command line or a network manager. When you wish to do this manually, you will need to look at the router that you are using. Generally speaking, routers will use their own methods to lock and bind IP addresses and you should always check the manual for the router that you are using. The way this works is by directly binding the MAC address to the IP address.

The MAC address is the media access control address—it is an identifier that is put into a device, uniquely defining it. This is permanent and assigned to the network interface controller (NIC) for that particular device. This means that the item will always have the same MAC address, no matter how many times it is directly factory reset or altered.

When you make the IP address static, what you do is directly assign that one particular MAC address to one particular IP address. This method will not be used to create a static IP for a virtual machine, however. In Kali Linux, creating a static IP address is incredibly simple. All you need to do is use the Network Manager settings. In doing so, you must go to the top right-hand corner of your screen and click on the menu arrow. Then, click on "Wired Connected" followed by "Wired Settings."

After you do this, you will be given a new window. You should see gear icons—click on the gear icon that is connected to the Wired menu. This will trigger another window to open, in which you will choose the IPv4 tab. You can then shift the IPv4 method from automatic to manual, followed by entering the desired static IP that you would like to implement. When you are choosing out the desired address, keep in mind that the first seven digits of your chosen address should match the default gateway. That is to say that if the router's gateway IP address is 123.456.7.8, your selected IP should have an address of 123.456.7.** and you should record that selected IP under Address under this menu. You must also select your netmask—for most people, simply entering 255.255.255.0 is good enough.

You must then record your Gateway, which should match the IP address of the router.

This leads to the following settings:

Address	Netmask	Gateway
•123.456.7.10 •Uses the first 7 digits of the Gateway and chosen ending	•255.255.255.0 •This by default.	•123.456.7.8 •Also the IP of the router.

Upon lining up these settings, you can then choose to set any DNS settings if you want them, though this is not necessary. After finishing setting up the address, netmask, and gateway, you can hit apply.

In order to ensure that you have the router's IP address, all you need to do is enter the command:

ip ro

If you look after the response "default via," you will have your router's IP address.

Lastly, to then apply all of the changes to the IP address, you must restart the network.

You can do so with the following command in the terminal:

sudo systemctl restart NetworkManager

Assuming you are already familiar with Linux and the basics behind using it, you know that sudo is the command that triggers the system to bypass any administrative restrictions, so long as you have been set as a sudo user. If you find that you are unfamiliar with this process, you may benefit from seeking out a beginner's guide to Linux before proceeding with the book.

With the sudo command entered, you can now stop to check your current local IP to make sure that your changes were received and made. You can do this with the following command:

ip a

You should then be able to see what the IP address on your system is. If it matches what you have tried to set, then you have been successful in setting your own IP address.

Protocol Layers

As briefly touched upon earlier, the internet is run by protocols. This protocol has five distinct layers that come together to create an internet protocol stack. The first four layers of the internet protocol stack are contained within the TCI/IP model. In understanding how these layers work, you are able to see exactly how people and systems interact with the internet as a whole. This section will introduce you to the layers of the internet as well as the methods of accessing them.

Internet Protocol (IP)

The Internet Protocol (IP) is the primary protocol dictating how communications are managed over the internet. It explains how datagrams, the information that your computer sends when requesting further information, are relayed across networks and boundaries. Its primary function is routing information, which then allows for information to be transferred, which then creates the internet as a whole. IP is tasked with transferring packets, small parcels of information that must be transmitted, from the source host to the destination host. It utilizes IP addresses in order to do so, providing them with the packets' headers. While the IP was once connectionless, it was also used as the basis of the Transmission Control Program that eventually became the Transmission Control Protocol (TCP). For this reason, you sometimes will see IP referred to as the TCP/IP, as will be discussed in the next section.

The IP began as IPv4 (Internet Protocol Version 4), though this is beginning to be replaced by IPv6. Ultimately, the IP is responsible for several functions. It can be divided into four distinct functions—the application, transport, internet, and linking of data. There is a fifth layer to the transmission of data and packages as well—the physical layer, though the TCP/IP model does not encompass the physical.

The TCP/IP Model

The TCP/IP model is one of the specifications of IP—it is the definitive list of rules on how communication should occur between computers on a network. It dictates the formatting standard for data, allowing all systems to utilize the same standards. Essentially, the TCP/IP model allows for all systems, no matter where they originate from, to access the same internet.

ISO/OSI		TCP/IP	
7	Application	Application	4
6	Presentation		
5	Session		
4	Transport	Transport	3
3	Network	Internet	2
2	Data Link	Network Access	1
1	Physical		

This is done by creating standard datagrams—these datagrams have two components. They have a header and a payload.

The header includes the source IP address, the IP address of the destination, and any other necessary metadata that will be needed to ensure that the information is all received exactly where it should be. The payload then is the data that will be delivered to the source that needs to receive it. When the payload and the header are nested together into what is referred to as a packet, the process is known as encapsulation.

With the IP stack, there are five distinct layers, as mentioned previously. The first four layers are relevant to the TCP/IP model. The first layer, the physical layer, is responsible for the encoding and transmission of data from one source to the proper network communications media. It uses data that is referred to as bits that get sent from the physical layer, which the destination's physical layer will receive. Essentially, the first layer takes the input you put into the computer, through clicks and presses of your keyboard keys in bits and encodes them. This

Next, you go through the data link layer—during this layer, the packets that were previously encoded are transferred from the network layer to two separate hosts. This transmission of packets is sometimes controlled by the software device driver in a network card or with firmware, and different protocols will have different methods of using this. In broadband internet, for example, access requires PPPoE as the necessary protocol, though a local wired network will utilize an Ethernet cord. Local wireless networks, on the other hand, will use IEEE 802.11 instead.

From the data link layer, you move on to the network or internet layer. This is where the data is actually taken from the source network and travels to the destination. It is typically achieved through passing the packet from network to network to network, a process referred to as internetwork, and this is where IP becomes relevant. This step involves data going from one source to the destination.

Once that data is sent to the destination, however, there are still two more layers before it can be accessed. The next layer is the Transport layer—its responsibility is to allow for the message to be transferred.

This usually occurs in one of two ways: either through transmission control protocol or through the User Datagram Protocol (UDP).

TCP as a system of communication refers to the connection-oriented communications protocol that is meant to allow for the exchange of messages across the internet. Usually deemed to be reliable thanks to the fact that there are several different error-checks to ensure that it all is translated and transmitted effectively.

It is first ordered into packets and numbered, and then the information is sent to the recipient and requiring a response back to the sender to confirm receipt of the message in the first place. If the receiver's response is anything other than accurate, then the message gets resent properly to ensure that the right data and packets are sent in a way that is properly read. This is the most common form of communication and transmission of data across the internet.

UDP, on the other hand, allows for faster transmission of data. Unfortunately, the faster transmission of data comes at a cost—accuracy.

Error checking is done away with, and it instead focuses on sending data as quickly and accurately as possible. Because waiting for the submission of data can take time, latency, or lag between what has been requested and what has been done occurs. In some instances, people may prefer to sacrifice accuracy and security in favor of the speed of UDP. Both of these protocols work through developing beyond the IP protocol—they effectively are sending packets of information to an IP address that has been sent via TCP or UDP.

Threats to Network Security

Of course, with the creation of networks comes threats as well. Nothing good can be left free from harm or problems, and data and network security are no exception. Every addition of an extra source or node can lead to weaker links—there are more holes that could potentially be prodded into. There are more chances of failure. And that is exactly what those who break into networks, hacking them or exploiting them, are looking for. They can pose a serious threat to network security, and it is important to know and recognize that.

There are several different forms of hacking and attempts to exploit technology, and this section will address some of them. A few of these may sound familiar from the previous chapter, while others are new. These are still not an extensive list of all the ways that it is possible to exploit or hack into a system, though they are important to understand. You cannot really understand networking if you do not understand the risk and threats as well.

Man-in-the-Middle

As discussed earlier in this book, the man-in-the-middle attack is an attack in which the attacker is secretly intercepting and sometimes altering the communication between a host and a recipient. The host and recipient think that they are able to communicate freely or that they are speaking directly with each other, but the MITM is listening—they are able to make two parties feel like they are safe and secure, all while gleaning valuable information that can be used later in some way, shape, or form. This usually is done through the attacker managing to gain access to one of the transmission IDs that are meant to be unique between the two end users.

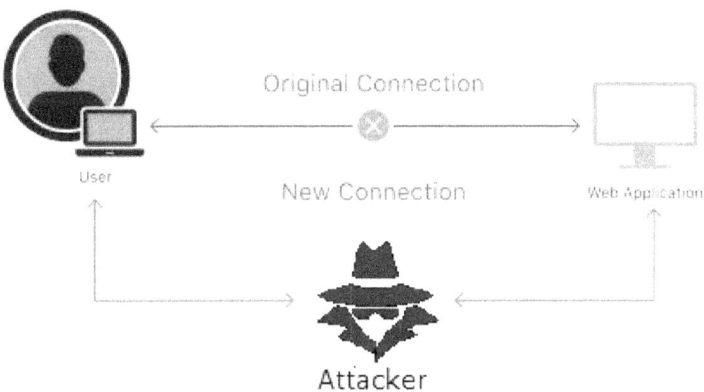

Sometimes, this occurs when someone within the Wi-Fi range is able to manage to insert him or herself into the connection and begin to intercept information back and forth. It is the most successful when the attacker is able to successfully impersonate both endpoints, making sure that neither person or user has raised any suspicion.

Cyberattacks

Cyberattacks are intentional malicious attempts to steal information or otherwise breach an information system of another person. Typically, it occurs because someone sees some sort of value in deliberately interfering with someone else's computer or network. The reasons for cyberattacks have been growing lately, with people sometimes seeing them as instant crash grabs—they may intentionally hack into a system in order to ask for a ransom or to offer to fix the discovered exploit for a price. No matter the situation, these cyberattacks are undeniably damaging. They can have serious financial implications while also putting sensitive data at risk. This can happen either actively or passively.

An active cyberattack involves someone intentionally trying to get into a system for some reason or to get something. The hacker is deliberately attempting to make changes to the system for some reason to the data that is either going toward or away from the individual. These include the use of masquerade attacks, such as the pretending to be an individual that has greater privileges that are actually granted or authorized in the first place.

A passive cyberattack, on the other hand, occurs when a network system is monitored and scanned to find open vulnerabilities. Instead of attempting to change the information in some way or otherwise alter the network, the information is simply used to monitor the data in some way. It is taken for use, but is not actually altered.

This is what someone would do if they intended to leak important information in order to blackmail or reveal something that otherwise would have remained private. Think of a hacktivist who would willingly use this information in order to reveal something.

DOS and DDOS

A denial of service attack is an attack designed to cause serious problems to the network. The entire purpose of this is to flood a specific network in order to crash it. Just as a traffic jam builds up when too many people are on a road that is too small to accommodate for it, the network will not be able to manage too many requests at the same time if it is not large enough to do so. Usually, this is done with an attacker machine able to run a client program, which then constantly inundates the targeted server with pings and requests in order to cripple it. As the network continues to try to respond in time, the network slows and slows until it eventually just stops altogether. DDOS (distributed denial of service) is exactly the same, though it makes use of several attacker machines rather than a single one. In doing so, larger networks can be compromised and crippled. Think about the implications of this happening—a website that needs to be functional will no longer be able to. A bank that has been crippled and cannot handle any traffic could risk people not being able to access funds. A hospital system that is unable to access and manage their patients' information would be unable to access records and medical histories or see whether people have recently had access to their necessary medication or other treatments. This sort of attack can be absolutely devastating, depending on the context.

MAC Spoofing

As you have already read, MAC addresses are usually permanent and hard-coded onto the NIC of a device. However, there are ways that this can be edited and altered. This is known as MAC spoofing. When MAC spoofing is used, the operating system being targeted or interacted with is able to be fooled to believe that the MAC address is actually something entirely different. Effectively, this allows for the identity of a computer to be altered and hidden. This is most often done because the individual wants to bypass the access control lists. If they have been banned from a server, for example, they are able to bypass this list by changing it. They can also impersonate another device in order to gain unauthorized access to a system through similar means.

MAC spoofing can also be done to conceal identity—if you wish to use an unencrypted connection, such as an IEEE encrypted line, you are not going to be able to prevent the Wi-Fi network from providing others with access to the MAC address. When you spoof your address, you are able to avoid being traceable. You will have hidden that identity and in doing so, you are able to be invisible, so to speak. Your true MAC address has been concealed and because of that, you can escape detection by law enforcement.

Chapter 11: Kali Linux: The Hacker Operating System

At this point, you should be able to see that cybersecurity is crucial and that there are very good reasons for learning how to both hack in order to identify any weak links in your systems and to protect them from harm. This is where Kali Linux comes in. Now, as a quick disclaimer before continuing, it is never recommended that you use these methods to deliberately damage or sabotage someone else or their connection. You should not be using the tools within Kali Linux for illegal purposes. However, if you do choose to do so, keep in mind that you will be entirely responsible for your own actions. This book does not condone, nor does it encourage the use of hacking for nefarious purposes. If you do decide to utilize these skills, the reason for doing so should be that you wish to protect or defend your own security.

This chapter will introduce you to Kali Linux properly—you will learn about what Linux is first and foremost, and from there, you will learn about Kali Linux, the specific distribution of Linux. You will be taught how to install Kali Linux, what Kali Linux comes packaged with, and some of the common Kali Linux specific information and commands that you may need to know. By the end of this chapter, you will have a working knowledge of what Kali Linux is as well as how to install it into your computer.

What is Linux?

First, you must understand what Linux itself is, as Kali Linux is ultimately a Linux distribution (colloquially referred to as a distro). If you are already familiar with Linux, you can skip this section, as it is not likely to provide you with anything else. If you are unfamiliar with Linux, please read through this section and remember that this is not a distribution to be taken lightly or to be treated as a toy. Kali Linux is dangerous and should not be in the hands of someone who is going to be unable to protect against serious damages.

Linux itself is an operating system—it is designed to be open-source. This means that the code itself is readily alterable and free to distribute. It is intentionally designed to be flexible and able to be changed in several different ways. The code is open-source, meaning access to altering the mainframe and base code is quite simple, and in many forms of Linux, if you are simply able to gain access to the terminal, you will be able to tell it to do anything—even if what you tell it to do is detrimental or risks crashing the entire system that you have installed.

When you learn to use Linux, you are given free control over the system. More specifically, however, Linux describes the kernel itself rather than the actual operating system. The kernel is the base that allows for the computer's OS to start up the hardware, allowing for the initial interaction between OS and user to begin building from that. Some forms of Linux, such as Mint or Ubuntu, are designed to be readily accessible, easily understood, and built to be managed and utilized with ease.

Other distributions of Linux are far more technical and require you to have much more programming knowhow in order to truly command them. These are distributions such as Gentoo, which is widely known as an internet meme much like deleting System 34 in Windows in order to cause the whole thing to crash. Other forms still bring with them several tools and functions that you may not necessarily have access to otherwise, such as several of the penetration-based tools of Kali Linux. It is important for you to understand what you can and cannot do, what your own capabilities are, and how you can possibly interact with the systems before you make it a point to install Kali Linux.

If thus far, you were lost with the talk of kernels and distributions or the idea of coding your own programs and commanding your computer, please stop reading now and seek out a beginner's book before revisiting. These concepts are crucial and it is expected that you have some level of familiarity with the system from here on out, whether you are a beginner or not. Remember that you can cause irreparable harm if you attempt to use this system without knowing fully what you are doing—you must be cautious and careful to avoid a disaster of your own doing.

What is Kali Linux?

Kali Linux is specifically a Debian-based Linux distribution. Developed by Offensive Security, Kali Linux was designed to be a leading trainer in information security professionals. With the tools utilized in Kali Linux, you are able to begin hacking with relative ease if you know what you are doing—it brings with it several of the tools that you will find necessary, and it also allows for training and certification.

In fact, if you wish to be an information security technician or professional, you are most likely going to be required to have a certification that you have earned based upon the courses taught by Offensive Security. When you have used Kali Linux, you are gaining access to the tools that are designed to help you with information security tasks. You will be able to engage in Penetration Testing, security research and more. Because Kali Linux is managed and maintained by Offensive Security, one of the leading trainers in cybersecurity, you know that the tools provided are much like the ones that you will be fighting in the future.

In particular, this distribution of Linux is designed to meet the needs of penetration testing professionals—because it is aimed toward professionals, it assumes that you already are familiar with Linux as an operating system.

Kali Linux boasts several important traits that make it useful in the hacking world—these tools make it valuable to both those interested in hacking for nefarious purposes and those who are interested in bettering security overall.

However, these traits came at a cost. Several of the commonly known benefits to using Linux distros in the first place have been changed in order to make Kali Linux a more valuable tool. After all, the beauty of Linux is that it is capable of anything that you are capable of programming so you are able to create an operating system that exactly serves the needs you have. Now, let's take a moment to go over those key changes from the standard Linux distribution.

It is single user root access.

Remember, root access refers to whether or not someone has administrative authority on that device. The root user has no safeguards, is not told any under any circumstances, and cannot be overridden by the system.

In most cases with various other Linux systems, it is strongly recommended that you avoid using the root access account and instead set up another with sudo privileges. However, that is not possible with Kali Linux—the OS does not allow for any other users or for root access to be left behind. This means that the operating system if you do not know what you are doing, can be completely destroyed with just one or two typos or not knowing what you are doing.

Because of the nature of the tools and usage scenario with Kali Linux, almost everything you will be doing would be considered higher privilege and you would either have to constantly sudo command the system, or you would need to remain in the root user account anyway. Because having to avoid the root account would be a burden, Kali Linux has instead shifted over to remain in root access constantly. This is yet another reason that this is not a distro for a beginner.

Kali Linux

- Single user root access
- Network services are disabled
- Linux kernel is custom and patched for wireless injection
- Repositories list is minimal for security

Network services are disabled.

While network services are usually enabled in Linux distros, within Kali Linux, there are system hooks that leave network services disabled by default.

This is a security method—it allows for services to remain secure and protects the distribution regardless of the packages that are installed. Other forms of networking, such as Bluetooth, are also disabled.

Linux kernel is customized.

While nearly every other Linux distribution is linked together by the common Linux kernel, the Kali Linux distro does not use that exact kernel—the one that is utilized in Kali Linux has been customized, allowing it to be patched for wireless injection, yet another way that it is able to act as a tool useful for penetration testing.

Repositories list is minimal.

Because Kali Linux is designed to be secure, there is a minimal list of sources for software that are allowed access to the system. While many people may feel the need or temptation to add systems that are not authorized or on the repository list, doing so can cause a high likelihood of crashing the Linux installation altogether. For this reason, you must recognize that Kali Linux is not so much a day-to-day OS as a tool to use for training and very specific usage scenarios. If you do not make use of it in one of these scenarios, such as penetration testing or practicing your skills, you are going to find little use for the system. You will not be using this for daily web browsing and attempting to answer emails or play video games—attempting to do so runs the risk of crashing the whole thing.

Should I use Kali Linux?

You may expect that a book written about Kali Linux would be spouting out all of the reasons that you should, in fact, use this distribution. However, due to the risks, the specialized and unique nature of this distribution, and the limitations that come with it, it is important to walk through the reasons that Kali Linux is likely not for you instead.

This distribution is designed specifically for professional testers and specialists. It is difficult to learn and it will not give you access to do anything you want.

Despite being open-access, it is only so open—there are aspects of this distribution that are locked due to security reasons, and you will not be able to change them. The packages in repositories, for example, must be signed by the committee, and these repositories are upstream. It is well-tested and the development team is one that can be trusted and respected. However, if you want a system that you have complete access to, Kali Linux is not for you.

Yes, there is some degree of customizability, but you will not be able to install juts anything. You must install from a chosen list of repositories if you wish to have them work right away. If you try to install something not on that list, you will have to go through several hoops to try to fix it up, and even then, you still are quite likely to cause more problems than you have fixed. For regular browsing and usage, Kali Linux is not right for you.

If you are already familiar with Linux and already are comfortable with network administration or system administration and want a tool to learn more, this may be the right OS, but this should never be treated as the first intro to Linux.

Especially because any unauthorized attempts to penetrate a network can not only cause significant damage but also carry hefty legal or personal issues, this should only be used by people that know what they are doing and are not likely to accidentally destroy someone else's network or access to service. Again, because it is so crucial to reiterate, if you are a beginner, seek out a Linux distribution that is designed to be easier—Ubuntu, Mint, and Debian are all fantastic starting points. Of course, if you are a penetration tester already or are actively studying penetration in order to become certified, Kali Linux is exactly right for you. You cannot beat the tools that are designed by professionals for professionals, nor can you beat the price of free for that toolset.

Kali Linux Features

If you have decided that Kali Linux is may be right for you, there are several tools that may be relevant to you. This section will guide you through the most common features of Kali Linux so you can begin to understand better whether this will be good for you to use.

Hundreds of Penetration Testing Tools

Kali Linux boasts a massive repository of tools that can be used for penetration testing, all of which have been verified and tested to be safe. Every tool provides a purpose that will be useful to your work in penetrating and controlling systems.

Free

This is perhaps one of the most compelling reasons to make use of Kali Linux—if it serves the right uses for you, it is absolutely free. You will never be required to pay to have access to this set of tools, meaning that there are no ongoing licenses to maintain.

Secure

Kali Linux has been developed by a small group that is trusted to interact with the repositories and even that has several protocols to help make sure that Kali Linux is as secure as possible. This means that any package that will be sent for download will be signed by developers who have committed and built it, allowing for tracking accountability if anything were to go wrong.

Customizable

While Kali Linux has very specific usage scenarios that are encouraged, and certain usages of the system are strongly frowned upon, the entire system has been built to be customizable.

You can try to change Kali Linux to suit your needs, even if those needs go against the recommended usage. You may run into complications, but you are able to attempt to do whatever you think you need to do.

Multi-Language Support

Unlike many other penetration tools, Kali Linux allows for true multilingual support. Instead of having to operate and learn everything in English, people are able to use Kali Linux in their own native language.

Open Source Git Tree

All source code is available for people to see or tweak to their specific needs. People can follow the development and source codes to make sure that they can get exactly what they want and need, with the few limitations listed in the previous section.

FHS Compliant

Kali Linux allows for Linux users to locate their files and libraries thanks to the familiar Filesystem Hierarchy Standard that has always been used. This means that if you are already familiar with Linux, using this has one less hurdle to get over.

Wireless Device Support

Kali Linux has been designed to support a wide range of wireless devices, allowing for it to be compatible with USB and other wireless devices with ease. This allows for easier access to information and transmission of information.

Custom Kernel

Because penetration testers need to be able to do wireless assessments, the Linux kernel within Kali will always be up to date with all of the latest patches to aid in the act of injection to other systems.

How to Install Kali Linux

At this point, you should have a good idea of whether installing Kali Linux will benefit you. If you think that it is, in fact, what is right for you after having looked through everything about the OS, then it is time to begin discussing the installation process of the OS. Installation is the first step toward being able to utilize the Kali Linux operating system and can be done in several ways. If you are installing Kali Linux in any way that is not traditional installation method of installing the Kali Linux OS on your computer or if you think that you will be running a virtual machine, you may be better off going to the official Kali Linux site and looking at the guides and tutorials that they have available.

What You Need for Installation

When you are ready to install, you must make sure that you have everything that you need. This can vary greatly depending on the system that you are using. Those running Linux probably already have everything that they need installed, but if you are running either macOS X or Windows, you are going to need to make sure you install the proper GPG for your particular operating system. Either way, if you go to the Kali Linux Kali Docs Official Documentation library, you will be able to go to the instructions for downloading the official Kali Linux images. Toward the bottom of the page, both links are provided for you to download the prover version of GPG.

After installing GPG, you need to download and import your copy of the official Kali Linux key. You will do this with the following command:

$ wget -q -O - https://archive.kali.org/archive-key.asc | gpg --import

In response, you will be provided with a key number. In order to verify that your key has been installed, you must try one more command:

gpg --fingerprint 44C6513A8E4FB3D30875F758ED444FF07D8D0BF6

So long as you do not run into anything telling you there is an error, you should see that you have a key as well as a time limit during which the key is effective.

Step 1: Getting official Kali Linux images

When you are installing your OS, you need an ISO file—this requires you to have a USB drive or a hard disk or some other method of interacting with the computer that you are installing Kali Linux on. You will need to have the image in either 32-bit or 64-bit format depending on the architecture of the system that you are using. When you need to know what system you are running and are currently on either Linux or OS X, you can enter a command in the terminal to get the result. You will enter in:

uname –m

and after doing so, you will get the response of either "x86_64," meaning that you are running a 64-bit format at the moment, or a response of "i386" meaning that you are currently running a 32-bit system. You need to make sure that the ISO that you choose is the right version.

On a Windows 10 system, you will need to press the **Start** button, followed by selecting **Settings > About**. In opening up the settings, you should see device specifications in the right.

There, you should be able to see whether your system is running either a 32-bit or 64-bit system.

You will be able to get the proper image in either .iso/.img files or in .torrent files. Keep in mind that doing so is specific to an Intel-based PC. You also have access to files that will allow you to run Kali Linux on a virtual machine, or in other formats as well. When you are downloading Kali Linux, make sure that you are always doing so from the Kali Linux official site run by Operational Security. Doing anything other than that can lead to serious problems as you no longer have a guarantee that the installation that you are currently running is safe and secure. You will need to ensure that the file you are downloading is secure if you are going to be using it to penetration test your own personal systems.

Step 2: Verify the Kali Image

Before going so far as to run Kali Linux Live, which will be discussed shortly, you need to double-check that you have the legitimate, official release of Kali Linux instead of some sort of hacked or altered version that was distributed elsewhere on the internet. You can do this quite simply in one of three different ways:

- Download an ISO image from the official Kali Linux "downloads" mirror and then calculate the SHA256 has while comparing it to the one listed on the Kali Linux site. You should be able to do this quite simply—but this is also potentially vulnerable to exploits.
- Download the ISO image through a torrent and it will also give you a file that has the calculated SHA256 signature on it. You are then able to use the shasum command if you are already on Linux or OSX, or in a tool on Windows to verify that the file's signature matches the signature within that other folder downloaded. Again, this suffers from potentially being vulnerable to exploit as someone could quite simply provide you with matching numbers just to make it look like a legitimate installation of Kali Linux in order to ensure that you are fooled.
- The only way to be as certain as possible is a bit more involved—you will need to download the cleartext signature file and the version of the file that was signed off with the official private key. Then, you must utilize GNU Privacy Guard. This will then verify that the SHA256 combination and the one in the cleartext files match, and then it will ensure that the signed version of the file with the SHA256 hash is also correctly signed with the proper official key.

Step 3: Create Kali Linux Bootable USB Drive

Perhaps the fastest method of getting Kali up and running is through using a live bootable USB. Essentially, what you are doing is getting Kali Linux onto a USB drive and then booting it up from that USB.

This comes with several advantages of its own, such as avoiding any sort of destruction or mayhem. When you use this, you are not making any changes to the system you are using—you are simply running it from the USB. This also brings up the point that it is portable and customizable—you will be able to take it with you anywhere and boot up from any computer, and you will be able to create your own custom Kali ISO onto the USB drive in the same way that will be discussed here.

In order to create the bootable drive, you will need to have a verified copy of the ISO, a disk imager utility (if you are using Windows, you can download the Win32 Disk Imager, or if you are on Linux or OS X, you likely already have this and all you will need to do is use the command, **dd** in order to pull it up) and a USB drive or an SD card, so long as the system that you are using allows for direct access with either of those methods. Your storage should have at least 4GB with more recommended.

Create the Bootable USB with Windows

When you do this on a Windows computer, you will have several steps to go through that are different compared to if you had been running a Linux or OS X machine.

- Attach the USB drive into any available USB port on the computer and note whichever drive designator has been set to it. With it mounted, launch Win32.

- Select the Kali Linux ISO file that you are imaging and confirm that you are overriding the proper USB drive. When you have confirmed that it is correct, press the Write button. As soon as it is finished imaging, eject the USB drive and it is now ready to use.

Creating the Bootable USB with Linux

On Linux, the steps are slightly more involved, and you run the risk of struggling or accidentally overwriting a disk drive that was unintended. You are going to need to make sure that you are using the right commands to guarantee that you are not accidentally overwriting anything.

- First, you must figure out the device path that you will be using to write the image to the USB drive. You want to do this *without* the USB inserted at that point in time. Within the terminal, you want to write:

    sudo fdisk -l

    You should get an output that shows a single drive with three partitions.

- At this point, plug in your USB to the available port and once again repeat the previous command of sudo fdisk -l and you should now get a similar output showing an extra device this time that was not there before—this time, that is your USB drive.
- Now, you must image the ISO file onto the USB device with a command similar to the one that will be provided below. This command assumes that your ISO image is named "kali-linux-2017.1-amd64.iso" and is currently within the working directory. It also assumes that your USB drive's name is "/dev/sdb" and you will want to replace the name of the file and the name of the drive if necessary. You can choose the blocksize if you wish to try to speed things up, but this is the safest size that has created reliable images. The command here is:

    dd if=kali-linux-2017.1-amd64.iso of=/dev/sdb bs=512k

- The imaging process can take upwards and sometimes over 10 minutes, so be patient as you wait for this process. You will not get any feedback about this process until the system is done.

- When it is finished, your USB device is now ready to boot.

Creating a Bootable USB on OS X

- Start with the USB drive unplugged. Open the Terminal and type the command:

    diskutil list

- You should see several device paths, just as with the Linux version. You will get information on each of the partitions and all of the information that you could possibly need.
- Now, plug in the USB device and rerun diskutil list again. Doing so will now present you with a new disk drive. You can now see a new disk drive that was not present before, which is how you now know how to address the command.
- Now, unmount the drive—this time, we will act as if the drive is named "/dev/disk6" for the example. Your command will be something like:

    diskutil unmount /dev/disk6

- At this point, you need to image the Kali ISO file to the device with a command such as:

    sudo dd if=kali-linux-2017.1-amd.iso of=/dev/disk6 bs=1m

    Keep in mind that there is no guarantee that your own file and drive will have the same file names. You will need to change them accordingly. Again, there will be no feedback until the drive is done loading, at which point you will have a bootable USB.

At this point, you will be able to use any of your USB drives to boot up the OS. All you need to do is bring up the boot menu upon starting your computer with the USB mounted and make sure you select Kali Linux. There are other methods that you can use to access Kali Linux, such as installing it onto your computer itself, but one of the most recommended methods of accessing the software is through the use of the USB drive.

If you have an interest in downloading the entire system onto your hardware, feel free to browse around the specific Kali Linux official website for more access and information to do exactly that.

Chapter 12: Basic Linux Commands

From this point on, the information you will be getting is a mix of practical information and information that you can actively use in some way. This chapter in particular will provide you with the necessary information to begin interacting with Kali Linux. You will be given a list of the most common and basic commands necessary.

As you read through these commands, try to really familiarize yourself with them. You want to make sure you understand what they are and how they can be best used to benefit you. If you are able to do so, you will ensure that you are also able to interact with your Linux distribution, no matter which you have chosen. Remember that with Kali Linux, you will be in root user by default and you will need to take the necessary precautions. When using several of these commands when you do not have root access, you run into problems that stop you from being able to move forward. However, with Kali, if you are already in the root user, the command is instantly carried out, even if it is a harmful one. This is why attention to detail, and a meticulous amount of it, is crucial if you really want to develop your skills with Kali Linux and become skilled at penetration testing and hacking.

The Terminal

If you are familiar with Linux and basic commands, you should also be familiar with the Terminal. This is the way that you are able to interact with the shell of Linux, commanding it to do what you expect. You are essentially going to be putting in input to the server and then expecting it to come out the other end with the proper response. This is the basis of the simplest Linux commands. As a quick refresher, if it has been a while, you will be emulating the terminal in a graphical environment so you can see the input and output in a way that you can read and understand.

If you already have Linux or OS X, you already have access to Terminal, and you can also install others. If you have Windows, you may want to install PuTTY. Kali Linux will also have its own terminal within it as well that you are able to access with ease.

Command Prompts

When you are interacting with the Terminal, you are using command prompts or shell prompts—you will likely see these used interchangeably as you read through various guides. When you are within the terminal, there is a very specific composition of the prompt that you will see. It will be the username of the user, the hostname of the server, the directory you are in, and the prompt symbol. In most cases, the prompt symbol that you will see is $.

Effectively, then, if you are nicknamed hacker as your user, and your server that you are on is hacking and you are currently in the default home directory, you may see a default prompt of:

hacker@hacking:~$

In Kali Linux, however, you are always logged onto the single root user account. You are going to see the username of "root" instead of "hacker" or any other name that may have been there.

Executing the Commands

When you want to give your commands then, you must specify what you want in a fashion that the system is able to manage properly. You can enter a script, a series of prescribed information that will trigger the system to respond in a specific way. You can also enter your own commands instead.

This is what the majority of this current chapter will be: ways to interact and command the server. When a command is running, it is called a process. When that process is happening in the foreground, you must wait for it to finish before you can do anything else. This is the default way to run the program.

You can also enter your commands in two forms: With or without arguments. When you enter a command without an argument, you are entering a simple command without expecting anything else. This will cause the computer to send you to exactly what you have specified or done exactly what you said. If you write **ls,** for example, you will suddenly get everything listed out in front of you on the screen—the current directory's files and directories.

However, an argument seeks to alter that command somewhat. In adding an argument, you add an extra condition—you may tell your system to bring up the files of a different directory. You may tell your system to shut down in 30 minutes instead of instantly. They add a change to the meaning of the original command. When you enter a command with arguments, you will enter it in a specific order of command, then the specification or location of what you are running.

Another common way that commands are executed is with options—this means that they have some sort of modification to follow. This is followed by a - and a letter that tells the system what you need from it.
For example, if we go back to **ls,** you may choose to add something else to it, such as **ls -l** which tells your system that you want it to list out a longer list of permission, including far more details than would ordinarily be included.

You can also mix and match, so you can have your options and arguments combined—in fact, it is incredibly common to mix the two together in order to run the right command. From here on, you will be provided with several commands within Linux that you will find to be useful. These will either be a great refresher course, or you did not need this information in the first place.

If you did not need this information, or you feel confident in your ability to navigate a Linux system, feel free to drop off here and skip to the next chapter. However, if you are not entirely confident in your ability to navigate through your software, it may be smart to at least spend the time to read over this comprehensive list of commands that have been provided for you. Of course, you can also always come back to this information later if you ever feel like you need a command and want to make sure that you are able to really learn how to use them.

Archives

The codes within this section are related specifically to the archive files within your system. They will help you to interact directly with archives, whether to access, move, or otherwise interact with them.

tar cf archive.tar directory This will create a tar file (archive.tar) that contains the directory.

tar cjf archive.tar.bz2 directory Similar to above, but the tar file will be compressed using the bzip2 format.

tar czf archive.tar.gz directory Another variation of the first command. It will create a gzip-compressed tar (archive.tar.gz).

tar xf archive.tar This is the opposite command of the above. It will extract the data from archive.tar.

tar xjf archive.tar.bz2 Use this to extract data from a bzip2 compressed tar.

tar xzf archive.tar.gz The command to extract from a tar that was compressed under the gzip format.

Directory Navigation

These codes will allow you access to moving around the directory quickly and easily. When you do this, you are able to shift around from space to space without having to manually go through your directories yourself one at a time.
It is easier to go through hit with the directory navigation.

cd You will be moved to the HOME directory.

cd .. It looks similar to the above, but has two periods. Will move you one level up the directory tree. For example, you are in directory 2, which lies within directory 1. You will move to directory 1 with this command.

cd /etc You will move to the /etc directory.

Disk Usage

These particular commands are directly related to disk usage. They will allow you to see all sorts of information about your current disk status, which can be incredibly necessary when you are monitoring your system closely.

df -h You will be able to see the used and available space on your disks with this command.

df -i Use this to see used and available inodes on your (mounted) filesystems.

du -ah Will bring up file size for all objects and directories in a human-readable format (bytes, megabytes, gigabytes).

du -sh Similar to the above, but will display the only the information from the directory currently being worked in.

fdisk -l When you need to see the partition sizes and types of your hard disks, use this command.

File and Directory Commands

The commands within this section will help you interact directly with the file and directory within your system. They will allow you all sorts of extra access and usability of your files and allow you to get the most out of your system and efficiency.

cp fileA fileB This command will copy over file A over to file B.

cp -r source_directory destination The command will copy over the directory recursively over to a selected destination. If the location already exists, the directory will be copied over. If the location does not exist, it will be created with a copy of the source directory files

ls -al Command will list all the files in a directory in a detailed format.

mv fileA fileB Renames fileA to fileB. It can also move a file. If fileB is a directory, the command will move fileA into said directory.

mkdir directory Makes a directory.

pwd Displays the directory you are currently in.

rm file Removes the file in question. Most commonly known as deleting a file.

rm -f file "Forces" the deletion of a file. No confirmation prompt will follow this command. Be sure you intend to delete this file.

rm -r directory Deletes a directory, along with its contents recursively.

rm -rf directory Use this when you want to "force" the deletion of a directory and its contents recursively. Again, be sure this is what you intend to do, as no confirmation will be asked.

File Transfers

These commands act as your guide to moving around files from place to place as necessary in order to ensure that you are always able to put your files where you want them.

rsync -a /home /backups/ Will synchronize the home directory over to /backups/home.

rsync -avz /home server:/backups/ Compression enabled synchronization of files or directories between a local and remote system.

scp file.txt server:/tmp Secure copies the file (in this case file.txt) to the /tmp folder on the server.

scp -r server:/var/www /tmp Recursively copies all directories and files from the server to the current system's /tmp directory.

scp server:/var/www/*.html /tmp Copies overall .html files from the server to the local /tmp directory.

Hardware Information Commands

These commands will provide you with all sorts of information about your hardware, ensuring that your hardware is functioning properly and effectively so you can be sure that all is well with your system.

badblocks -s /dev/sda This will check to see if there are any unreadable blocks on the disk sda (you can change sda to whatever disk drive you want to check).

cat /proc/cpuinfo This will provide you with the current CPU information, such as usage, speed, and other important aspects of its ability to run.

cat /proc/meminfo This will provide you with memory information, such as usage, speed, and other important aspects of its ability to run.

dmidecode This will show you pertinent hardware information from the BIOS.

dmesg This will show messages in the kernel ring buffer.

free -h This will display the free and used memory space in your system at that moment, specifically in a human-readable form. You can also select to -m instead of -h for the display in MB, or -g to get your result in GB.

hdparm –I /dev/sda This will provide you with all sorts of information about the disk sda.

lspci -tv This shows you the current PCI devices.

lsusb -tv This shows your current USB devices.

Installing Packages

These commands are all about installing packages from your files, whether from zip files, downloaded files, or otherwise.

rpm -i package.rpm Installs the package from a local file, in this case named package.rpm.

tar zxvf sourcecode.tar.gz

cd sourcecode

./configure

make

make install As opposed to installing from a package, this will have you install software from source.

yum info package Displays information about the package you reference.

yum install package Installs a package.

yum remove package Uninstalls (removes) a package.

yum search keyword Provides a search for a package using a keyword.

Networking

These commands are directly related to networking—allowing you to see what is going on with your own network and anything that your own network is interacting with.

dig domain Displays the DNS information for a given domain.

dig -x IP_ADDRESS Use this to run a reverse lookup of a given IP address

ethtool eth0 A tool to view and change network drivers and hardware settings.

host domain Displays the DNS IP address for a given domain

hostname -i This command is used to displaying the network address of the "host name".

hostname -I Very similar to the above command, but this will display all *local* ip addresses.

ifconfig -a This will bring up all network interfaces and their ip addresses.

ifconfig eth0 Will display the eth0 address and its details.

netstat -nutlp Will show oyu any listening tcp & udp ports and their related programs.

ping host Will send an ICMP echo request to "host".

wget http://domain.com/file Downloads the web file found at the given web address.

whois domain Will display the *whois* information for "domain".

Performance Monitoring

These commands are dedicated to ensuring that you are able to monitor your system's performance. This will make sure that your system is functioning well, effectively, and to your preference in order to ensure that there is nothing further you have to do to optimize your own settings to what you want or need them to be.

htop This will allow you to move to the top of the process viewer.

iostat 1 This will allow you to see the input/output statistics.

lsof Allows for a list of all open files currently presents on the system.

lsof -u [username] Allows for a list of open files present currently by the username specified.

mpstat 1 This will allow you to see processor-related stats.

tail 100 var/log/messages This will let you see the last 100 system log messages.

tcpdump –i eth0 This will allow you to see all packets on that particular interface listed (in this case, eth0).

tcpdump –i eth0 'port 10' This will allow for the monitoring of data on port 10, and you can change the port name to whichever port you are trying to manage.

top This will show the top processes and allow you to manage them.

vmstat 1 This will allow you to see the virtual memory-related statistics

Process Management

These commands are dedicated to process management—they tell you what the processes that are currently ongoing are doing, as well as allow you to shift from foreground processes to background processes as needed to make sure that your own activity does not suffer due to other processes running as well.

bg Will show background tasks or those that have stopped.

fg This command will push the most recent background process to the foreground.
fg n Similar to the above command, this will push process "n" to the front.

htop Will allow you to interactively monitor your computer's processes.

kill pid Use this to end or "kill" a particular process, where the process ID matches "pid".

killall processname When you want to kill all processes with a particular name, utilize this command.

program & This starts your selected program in the background.

ps Displays your own processes currently running.

ps -ef Displays *all* of the processes currently running in the system.

ps -ef | grep processname This will display the information for "processname".

top A process viewer. It is older than *htop*, but serves the same purpose. It has some differences, such as lack of mouse support (something *htop* has). Pick your preference.

Search

When you need to find something within your system, these commands are your best bet. When you are using your search commands, you will be able to find the files you need quick access to with ease and learn exactly where they are so you are able to jump to them and access them elsewhere.

find /home -size +25M Utilize this command to find files larger than 25MB in /home

find /home/mark -name 'prefix*' This will find files in /home/mark that start with "prefix".

grep pattern file This will look for pattern in "file".

grep -r pattern directory Performs a recursive search for pattern in "directory".

locate name Will look for files and directories by the specified "name".

SSH Logins

ssh host Connects to host using the username you use locally.

ssh user@host Connects to host as "user".

ssh -p port user@host Connects to host using port.

System Information Commands

These commands are all used for some sort of system information to understand what the system is doing and how you are able to interact with it. These are Linux specific—they should work for any form of Linux you are operating within, Kali Linux included. Some of these commands may be less useful on Kali Linux, but they are important to know anyway when interacting with other Linux systems. Consider this your sort of refresher course on how to interact with Linux.

cal This will show you the current month's calendar.

cat /etc/redhat-release This shows you which redhat is currently present on your computer for use.

date This will show you the current time and date on the system you are using.

hostname This will tell you what the name of the system host is.

hostname -I This will provide you with the host's IP address.

last reboot This will show you the last time that the system was rebooted.

uname -a This allows for the display of the Linux system's information that is stored.

uname -r This allows for the output to show which kernel release you are using.

uptime Tells you how long your system has been up or how long it has been loading.

w This will show you who is currently online on the system.

whoami This will tell you who you are currently logged into the system as.

User Information and Management Commands

These commands are crucial to your ability to managing user information. When you master these controls, you can add and remove people from your server. You can make sure that certain people have certain permissions, and more. These commands may not be so necessary within Kali Linux, where you are designed to be in root user and not others, they are still fantastic to know and understand.

groupadd group1 Allows you to create a new group "group1" in this instance. You can replace "group1 with any other name for your group.

id shows the user and group ids of the current user on the system.

last Shows who the last people that logged on were.

useradd −c "full name" −m "nickname" Allows for the creation of an account with the comment of "full name" and the home directory of "nickname".

userdel "name" allows you to delete the user "name".

usermod −aG group1 "name" Allows you to move user "name" to the "group1" group.

Part II

Kali Linux Hacking

Chapter 13: Nmap and Detecting and Exploiting Vulnerabilities

At this point, you may be quite eager to get started with Kali Linux once and for all. You should now have the OS installed yourself, or you are preparing to do so. Either way, reading through this section can provide you with valuable information. This is where you begin to see the true power of Kali Linux and how it can be used. You will begin to see the strength that can be earned in hacking and in learning to see and wield that strength for yourself, you should also be able to begin to see just how easy it is for a network to go unprotected or undefended. When this happens, it is in your best interest to ensure that you can figure out vulnerabilities in order to patch them up.

Nmap is just one of many tools that Kal Linux offers, and this particular chapter focuses on it. Nmap is powerful, allowing you to gather and identify information that is meant to be useful, allowing you to detect everything on the system. It is primarily a security tool, but you should keep in mind that it can be used to cause harm as well. Now, it is time to dive into the beginning of the actual hacking process. If you have already installed Kali Linux, go ahead and open it up—Nmap comes by default, already provided within the system.

What is Nmap?

Nmap stands for network mapper—it is an incredibly popular tool that is used to discover that is available to you. As with all of the tools provided to you within the Kali Linux distribution, this is free to use and secure. When you use Nmap, you are able to map out networks, allowing yourself to see inventories and find open ports as well. It is quite simple to use—it brings up a terminal that you are able to enter your commands and scripts within, allowing you to do whatever you would like within the system once you have gotten in.

This tool is able to work through firewalls and routers, it can bypass an IP filter, and it is able to navigate into systems. While it was designed to be capable of getting through massive networks, it can also be used on smaller scales as well. It is primarily used for port scanning, version detection, operating system detection, and using ping sweeps. It works quite simply—it uses IP packets in order to find hosts on a network and what they are running. Plenty of information can be earned just by finding out what someone's computer is running on.

Overall, Nmap is incredibly powerful—it enables you to do all sorts of actions and search for several exploits. It not only gathers information but also allows for the scanning of security, making it a multipurpose tool that can greatly benefit you.

It can be used for actions such as:

- Detecting any live hosts on a network
- Detecting any open ports that are currently present on the host
- Detecting OS, hardware, and software
- Detecting vulnerability through Nmap scripts

The tool itself is incredibly common and it is also compatible both with CLI and GUI, meaning it is not only common and powerful, but also flexible.

How to Use Nmap to Understand and Exploit Vulnerabilities

When you are ready to use Nmap, you have several different options. You will be able to scan one target, limited targets, or several targets, all based on the command that you are able to submit. The target determines exactly how you would go through the process of using this system, but ultimately, doing so will take some time.

Scanning Commands

Perhaps the most basic usage of Nmap is through scanning. When you want to scan, you have several different options. You can choose what you wish to target, whether it is one individual, several individuals, or an entire directory. Imagine for a moment that you want to scan a single unit or system. You would do so with the following command, changing the IP addresses accordingly.

nmap target
nmap target.com
nmap 192.143.1.1

This will scan that one specific system. If you wish to scan all associated subnets to that system, your command will change slightly.

It would instead be:

nmap target/cdir
nmap 192.143.1.1/24

And if instead, you wanted to scan several different targets instead, you would simply label them and separate the IP addresses with spaces. For example, maybe you would write:

nmap target target1 target2
nmap 192.143.1.1 192.141.1.2

You even have the option to scan only several IP addresses in a row without scanning the entire subnet. When you wish to scan 50 of the associated IP addresses but not the entire subnet, you will use the following command:

nmap target-50
nmap 192.143.1.1-50

This would then lead to the scanning of every IP address from 192.143.1.1 to 192.143.1.50 all in one go.

You may also decide that what you need is a list of several hosts that are being scanned—in this case, you want to add the proper parameter. In this case, that parameter would be **-sL**, which would create the command prompt of:

nmap -sL target/cdir
nmap -sL 192.143.1.1/24

Sometimes, however, you may want to scan the entire subnet, but you also know that you need to leave a section of that subnet entirely unscanned in order to avoid detection. Especially if you have the single IP address that you must avoid, you can then create your code with a parameter meant to exclude that one IP address. This is quite simple. All you need to do is add in the **-exclude** parameter like so:

nmap 192.143.1.1/24 - -exclude 192.143.1.13

You can even enter a single file that contains all excluded IP addresses if you have one, inserting the file name within the exclusion instead.

Your scanning can even get more specific as well—you can start to specify exactly which ports are to be targeted if you have the right codes as well.

Scanning Techniques and Commands

Of course, there are other types of scans that you can perform as well. Nmap has several different scanning techniques available that will be necessary for you to know to be effective. This section will provide you with the information you will need to use several other scan types as well.

TCP SYN Scan

Commanded with the prompt **-sS** the TCP SYN scan is a basic scan. It is commonly referred to as half-opening because it gathers information from the remote host without finishing the TCP process that was discussed earlier in this book.

In this sort of scan, Nmap seeds out an SYN packet to the right destination but never bothers to actually create or trigger a session. In the end, the interaction never gets logged by the target computer because the computer never initiated a session. This is what makes TCP SYN scanning so beneficial. This is used by default, though you will need root access. Of course, if you are using Kali Linux as you do this, there will be no problem, as you will be in the root account by default. A command for this sort of scan looks like:

nmap -sS 192.143.1.1

TCP Connect() Scan

When the SYN scan cannot happen for any reason, this will be the default scan that is used. With the code of **-sT** in order to utilize this scan, your system will instead complete the TCP handshake process, requiring the other system to log the transaction. This is only good for finding TCP ports rather than any others .To use this code, you would have a command such as:

nmap -sT 192.143.1.1

UDP Scan

This scan seeks out open UDP ports in whatever the targeted machine is. It does not make use of an SYN packet due to the targeting of a UDP port instead. However, you are still able to make this more efficient if you use the –sS and –sU commands together.

In using this scanning method, Nmap sends out a UDP packet and waits for some sort of response. An error message implies that the port is closed, but a proper response will let you know that the port is actually open and accessible. In this case, you will use the following command:

nmap -sU 192.143.1.1

FIN Scan

Sometimes a TCP SYN scan would not necessarily be the right choice based on the parameters that you have been provided. Usually, a firewall will cause a block from the SYN packets, so you will need to go through another method.

When this happens, you can try to make use of a FIN scan—this only sends a FIN flag, meaning it does not require the completion of the TCP transaction that would otherwise trigger the detection of Nmap. The proper command for a FIN scan is –sF such as:

nmap –sF 192.143.1.1

Which then brings back plenty of information—it should provide whether the host is up or down, what the latency is, and the state of the port. The target does not log this scan, but you are able to get the information.

Ping Scan

Unlike the other forms that have been discussed thus far, ping scanning is only used to determine if the host is currently alive or active. It does not discover whether a port is open. It does require root access, as there is the potential to send out ICMP packets. When there is no root access granted, it will complete the command using connect() call.

The command for a ping scan is -sP and it would be used:

nmap -sP 192.143.1.1

Version Detection

This is the command you need if you want to determine what kind of software is being used on the target computer or any ports. It does not detect any open ports, though it does need to get the information from any open ports in order to provide the information on the software that has been detected. The first step here would be to find a port that is open with a TCP SYN scan and then direct the –sV to the specific port available.

nmap –sV 192.143.1.1

Idle Scanning

In an idle scan, you are able to maintain your invisibility while scanning. In this particular technique, you do not send out any real packets from your own IP address. Instead, it takes a host from within the target network in order to send out packets. This will require you to first figure out an open port within the IP and then uses a zombie host in order to communicate with the target. In this code, you will use first the IP of the zombie host and then the IP of the target in order to create a command of:

nmap -sI 192.143.1.4 192.143.1.1

In this instance, the zombie host of 192.143.1.4 is being used to communicate with 192.143.1.1 without detection since they are a part of the same network.

Penetration Testing

Ultimately, penetration testing can be broken down into seven steps or phases—when you are able to get through these phases, you are more likely to find some sort of weakness or vulnerability. In utilizing these phases, you will find that your own ability to break through a system grows.

You will be more likely to crack through, which means that you are more likely to identify any of those weaknesses that you need to patch in your own system. The phases of penetration testing are pre-engagement, reconnaissance, threat modeling, exploiting, post-exploit, report, and re-test. You will be guided through each of the steps during this section of this chapter.

Pre-Engagement

This particular step is more like a precaution, but it is crucial—when you are in the pre-engagement stage, you need to begin by figuring out the test's scope. Essentially, you are looking for the exact goals of your attempt to penetrate the network. You need to ensure that you know what you are planning out so you do not do anything unintended. Especially if you will be performing this as a possible career path, you need to get into the habit of laying out what you are going to do and what the limits on what you are and are not allowed to do are.

You need to know exactly what is expected for you to do and which networks you should be focused on. Note it all down. If you are trying to crack into someone else's network at their behest, make sure you cover yourself legally and get signed documentation stating that you are working at their request and within their terms. Because penetration testing is dangerous by virtue of it attempting to chip away at security measures, you want to make sure that you are safe from being blamed if something were to go catastrophically wrong, which can occasionally happen.

Reconnaissance

At this stage, you are going to work on gathering information. While you may prefer to skip over this if you can get away with it, you are going to be more prepared if you actually know what you are doing. When you have the information that you need all lined up neatly in front of you, you will know what you expect. In particular, you may want to gather information about the network you are targeting or the most likely types of technology you will be encountering. You may want to have personal information about the people that you are trying to hack into, or about their email addresses.

When you are trying to sneak into a network, you never know what is and is not helpful or necessary. Gather as much information as you possibly can in order to be prepared and then move on to step 3, only after you are content that you have gathered anything that will be useful to you.

Threat Modeling and Identifying Vulnerabilities

Step 3 is still all about planning—at this point, you want to take all of the information that you have gathered in the previous steps and begin brainstorming up what the most realistic vulnerabilities and threats that the network would face would be. Does it use a certain network type that is particularly vulnerable to a specific plan of attack? Is there an exploit on the type of hardware they are using? Anything goes here, so long as it is a relevant threat that the target will likely face.

This stage can also utilize a vulnerability scanner in order to scan the network for weaknesses. This could be done to find any vulnerabilities that are currently within that particular network, allowing you to calculate out the most likely vulnerabilities present. This can be a fantastic asset to you when you are trying to understand how best to access the network that you are attempting to penetrate. Kali Linux, luckily, comes with Metasploit—a way that you can scan for vulnerabilities within a list of specific target IPs. Metasploit will be discussed in-depth later within this book.

Another common technique at this stage is to use scanning tools and port scanners in order to find open ports or live hosts. In doing so, you may find that you are able to find another weakness that can be exploited to gain access. This technique allows you to scan devices, allowing for another point of entry.

This is almost like reconnaissance v 2.0—here, you are making it a point to get more details about the systems. You should be able to identify what systems are present, whether or not they are currently up and active, or whether there are any sorts of firewalls or antivirus software installed. With your list of vulnerabilities identified, it is time to start figuring out more information as well.

Can you get any valuable information form looking at the employees on the network? Is there value in finding customer data? Do customers have access to symptoms? Is there a possibility to steal financial information? If there is, then it is quite possible that you may want to look somewhere other than surrounding the financial information first, in an effort to sneak around and figure out a better plan of attack rather than trying to run in, guns blazing, straight into a trap or an area that is heavily guarded. Think about the most likely possibilities in this situation and come up with a tentative plan of attack, but remember that your test is most likely going to be constantly evolving and changing as you get more and more information.

Exploitation

At this point, it is time to begin attempting to access the network. You should have several different locations that you could use to attack the system and it is time to begin making those moves. Have you found any weaknesses that can be used to access? You may try to start a shell, or try to get some sort of credential assigned to you so you can begin to access as a root user instead. Is there any room for using another computer's information to help you get head? The main part of this phase is attempting to gain as much access as you can without being detected and blocked out. While it is possible to do plenty of damage without ever actually gaining administrative accesses and permissions, most of the time, what you are attempting to do is get that permission. This stage will be largely dependent upon the network that you are attempting to break through, and you will need to be creative. Make sure that you document what does and does not work as you go so you can start to figure things out. Remember, if you are doing this for yourself or for a client, you are going to want to know exactly what worked and what did not. When you have gotten as much information as you can here, it is time for the next stage.

Post-Exploitation

Next comes the post-exploitation phase. At this point, you will have finished testing, either due to running out of tie or having reached the end of your ability to exploit or run out of the system to exploit. At this point, you must make a list of all vulnerabilities and provide them to the client. As you have gone through, you should have made notes, or potentially screenshots, of anything that did or did not work. You should be able to figure out how significant the exploit that you have done is—did you get into the main server or did you get stuck at a computer with little sophisticated access to the server? How valuable was the information that you got from the system, if any? How at risk is the system itself?

Beyond that, you should also be thinking of how to fix any vulnerabilities that were discovered. Can you think of an easy patch to solve the problem? Is there something else that you can do to ensure that the network is more secure?

What can the network do better? What worked well? Beyond that, you should also make sure that you clean up as well. You need to remove anything that was planted within the system and change back any and all settings to what they used to be. You want to make sure that everything that you have exploited is removed.

Reporting

At this stage, it is time to come up with your report. It may not be fun, but if you have gone through the penetration testing in order to help someone, you need to make sure that your report is written up nice and neatly. This is where you are able to convey any weaknesses and vulnerabilities that will put the client at risk. You will make sure that you are able to tell them which exploits happened and how they should be fixed.

This stage should be as brutally honest as possible—you want the other party to know exactly what happened and how to fix it. If their system is truly that vulnerable to exploitation and you were able to get access to everything, let it loose. Tell them in unbiased but honest terms exactly how things went wrong. This is where they are also given an example plan of action to make sure that everything gets patched up. The clearer you make this stage for the client, the better you will be at your job and the more likely it will be that your client is able to fix the problems and secure the network.

Retesting

This is not a stage that everyone is willing to go through as penetration testers, but it is an important one if you want to do a thorough job in doing so. During this stage, you will give the client time to look through their own vulnerabilities and attempt to repair them and you reevaluate their attempts to bolster their defenses. You will essentially retest the parts that were fixed in order to see that they actually did patch up any vulnerability that was there. You may not always be asked to do this, but if you are, it is always an act of good faith to go through with it.

Chapter 14: How to Become and Remain Anonymous

Anonymity is crucial if you hope to be a hacker, no matter the kind. If you are not careful, it becomes incredibly easy to simply blacklist your specific IP address and you no longer have that access. Instead of managing to get through the system or finding any exploits, you instead end up banned and unable to do anything. However, that does not have to be your fate if you are trying to hack—you can instead cover your tracks.

Just as many burglars will wear gloves in order to hide their fingerprints from the system that they are trying to access, making sure that you put on your own metaphorical digital gloves can help you remain anonymous. This means that your information will be private—you will be able to disguise yourself and your software in order to make sure that your real IP address is not being used.

Now, you may be thinking, what if you are using a virtual machine? Would that not have a digitized IP address or be hidden more because the entire thing is digital? Yes and no—however, that is still only as secure as the network that you are using. This means that if you really want true anonymity, you are going to want to involve the usage of something else as well. You are going to want to add in extra tools and precautions to arm yourself against your IP address is found out. When you are able to fight it off, you are more likely to remain anonymous. There are several tools out there that would be able to aid you with the process of being anonymous and protecting yourself, all built within Kali Linux and ready to be used. All it will take is the time and effort to configure everything, but it will be well worth the effort.

The three methods in particular that will be discussed within this chapter will be proxy servers, VPNs, and the use of TOR. Within each section, you will be guided through what the particular method is, how it works, and how to use it with Kali Linux.

Proxy

- Obscuring the IP address through disguising them

VPN

- Creating an extra layer between your own personal IP address and the internet for security

Tor

- Having your digital footprint constantly shifted from place to place around the world to hide your trail

Proxychains

Perhaps one of the simplest methods to obscure your IP address is through the use of a proxy server. Through using chains of proxies, you are able to obscure your tracks, making them harder to follow. In making them more difficult to follow, you will be more likely to avoid detection. When you use a proxy, of course that proxy is logging your information. However, you can get around this as well—you can string together several proxies together in a chain. So long as at least one proxy is able to be outside of the jurisdiction of the target, you should be able to avoid the problem altogether.

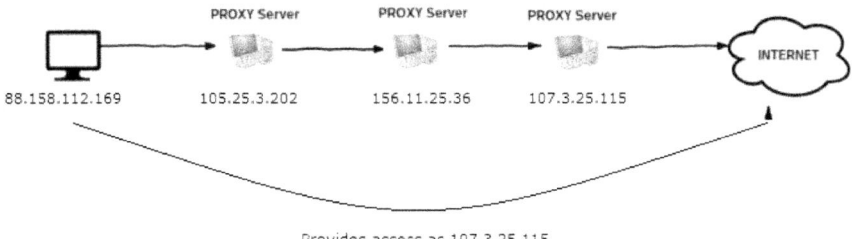

Luckily, within Kali, you have access to a tool known as Proxychains. This can be found within your directory, which you can pull up with a location command. It will most likely be in the /usr/bin directory.

When you are using Proxychains, you will be using a very straightforward command:

proxychains [enter command that is proxied] [add in any arguments]

Now, imagine that you wanted to use this with Nmap to scan anonymously and through a proxy. Perhaps in particular, you want to use a TCP SYN scan on the IP address 192.143.1.1 but you want to do so through a proxy utilizing the tool. In this case, you would create a command prompt of:

proxychains nmap -sS 192.143.1.1

This then triggers you to do the TCP SYN scan on that one particular IP address through a proxy.
With the syntax understood, you are able to move on to completing a config file. As with basically anything else within Linux, there are simple text files known as config files that will hold all of the necessary information. You are able to open these in any of the text editors you have, such as via gedit or leafpad.

Open the config file into your text editor and you should see a file with all sorts of information. Within it, you will find that one particular area has a spot for you to add the proxy. You will simply enter the IP address of any proxies that you are utilizing there. Typically, proxychains will default to Tor, as you can see within your file. If you will be using Tor, leave this as is. If you are not using Tor, you will need to make the appropriate edits to the file. This book will be moving forward with Tor.

With the proxy server set up, it is time to test it. You can do so by sending out a scan through the proxy. When you send the scan out, you should see your chosen IP address listed and it should line up with your proxy one.

Beyond just setting up the proxy, however, you can do plenty of other things with this as well. You can add several proxies, for example, and then chain them together so they chain either at random, in a specific order, or uses only part of them.

Start by opening your proxychains config file again. You will then look at the dynamic_chains line—you can see that it is commented out.

This means that it will not be used at this moment. If you erase the comment mark, it should activate when the process is run. You can also find random chaining as well within your file. You can re-add the # to comment out the dynamic_chains line and instead remove the # from the random_chain option instead. You can only make use of one or the other of these options at any given time, so you will have to go back in and remove one if you wish to use the other.

VPN

Another layer of security that you can add to your system is through adding a VPN on top of the use of proxy addresses. This is common practice—it allows for further protection from piracy or other issues. It also allows people to bypass, for example, any particular activities that may be illegal within a country. It also can allow you to scan other networks without being detected—something else that is commonly considered to be illegal in several countries. Even just scanning the network can be enough to lead to it being considered illegal, even though you may not have done anything with it.

Now, since you are currently reading about how best to do exactly that, you are going to find that the extra security is crucial to protecting yourself.

There are several reasons to use a VPN, all of which are incredibly compelling. Not only does a VPN allow you to cloak your IP address and therefore protect you, but it also allows you to use any network while ensuring that there is still encryption. Further, you will be able to log into your sensitive information without worrying about it being hijacked if you are on another network. You will be able to skip past any monitoring that may have been installed, or access region-restricted websites.

Of course, it is also important to recognize that your VPN will not cloak everything—there will be some ways to identify you. For example, your regular search engine can probably recognize you simply due to cookies and browsing behavior, especially if you are already logged into an account with that particular engine. Despite the shortcomings, however, the fact that a VPN can help you hide more means that you can rely on it to provide you with more protection than you would otherwise have. Just as a seatbelt is not a guarantee of safety in a car accident, a VPN is not a guarantee of security—however it is an extra layer that is there to help keep you safe if necessary.

When you want to enable a VPN on Kali Linux, you will have a handful of commands to use and steps to follow, but in the end, you will add extra protection to your software, meaning that you will be able to better protect yourself.

Step 1: Enable VPN

The VPN option is usually disabled by default when you use Kali Linux, so you will have to open it up before continuing. This will require you to enter your own command, such as:

apt-get install network-manager-openvpn

This particular command is specific to enable a VPN. At this point, you may need to restart your networking and network-manager. Upon the restart, you should find that the VPN is now available.

Step 2: Download and extract openvpn

Now, you will need to download the openvpn.zip file. This is not particularly difficult—a code such as:

wget https://www.privateinternetacess.com/openvpn/openvpn.zip

To download the file. Once it is downloaded and saved, you will then need to unzip the file and make sure it is deposited into the right directory for later use. You can do this with the following command:

unzip -q openvpn.zip –d /etc/openvpn

Your file should be ready, and now it is time to move on to step 3.

Step 3: Configure Network Manager to use PIA VPN

At this step, you will be setting up Network Manager so it will recognize and allow the use of the VPN that you are hoping to set up. This will involve you going into Network Manager, editing the connections, then swapping to the VPN tab and selecting that you would like to add it. You would then click on ADD, at which point, you would then set the type as OpenVPN. Then, click on create.

If you go to VPN, you will find several important details that will allow you to tell whether or not you are actually using the proper VPN in the first place.

In this case, you should see a connection name of PrivateInternetAccess VPN, a gateway that should be closest to your own personal location, a username that you can set in, a password that you can save, and then the CA certificate.

To get the CA certificate, you must go to /etc/openvpn in order to access the right directory, and then select on ca.crt to use it within this stage.

Now, click on **Advanced** and choose the box that is next to **Use LZO data compression.** You then must click on **OK,** then save and close the window.

At this point, if you click on Network Manager > VPN Connections > PrivateInternetAccess VPN, you should see a yellow connection indicator. Your VPN is now ready for use.

Tor and Kali Linux

Tor is yet another layer in the security umbrella that you can create in order to ensure that you are able to protect yourself. This is just another security precaution, but if you make good use of it, you can find that you are actually able to really protect yourself, especially if you begin to layer these safety methods together to protect your anonymity as much as possible. Remember, Kali Linux is already secure, but you are able to add extra layers to it utilizing the tools within its repository. Tor is another of those particular tools that are able to help protect you that comes with the Kali Linux toolset.

Tor itself is free software and will protect you through actively bouncing your communication throughout several different network points. Essentially, there is a massive network created by volunteers around the world.

They help transfer your information erratically so it cannot really be tracked easily. In constantly bouncing your information from place to place, you essentially end up with your data being highly protected. Your history will not be easily tracked and the sites that you are visiting are not able to know exactly where you are physical.

Effectively, you block yourself from being seen because people all over the world send your signals and information all over the place. One request may originate in the United States while another pops up in Spain and another in Germany.

Especially if you layer this with the previously discussed methods for real anonymity, you become incredibly difficult to track. You would not only have a series of different IP addresses being cycled through, but you would also have those IP addresses encrypted and protected by your VPN, and then you would further have protection because your access to the internet is being passed through Tor instead of through your usual methods.

When you want to use Tor on your Kali Linux machine, you will have to install it manually. Because you are on Kali, you are locked into being the root user, which means that you cannot use the shortcut mode that you are usually able to utilize. Instead of being able to utilize any shortcuts, you will need to manually download the Tor download. You can do this through the Tor Project official website. You will want to get the bundle download from their website and then download the torbrowser-launcher from GitHub. Make sure that you download the architecture appropriate files and save it somewhere that you are able to access. Then, utilizing the **tar** command, you should extract the package from the download directory. You can do this with the following command:

 # tar –xvf tor

Keep in mind that this command believes that the only file within your directory that begins with "tor" is your file for the tore download. Then, you need to run the Tor Browser Bundle. This will require you using the start-tor-browser script that you have just extracted:

 # ./start-tor-browser.desktop

In doing so, you will see Vidalia launched, and that will connect to Tor. With Tor connected to, Firefox will launch. If you are able to utilize these three different methods for privacy in tandem, you may quickly find that you are actually able to protect yourself greatly from the risks out in the real world of the internet. You will be able to ensure that your IP address is not as likely to be discovered, especially if you are messing around with some of the particular interests of those using Kali Linux, such as penetration testing that may otherwise become problematic.

Chapter 15: Metasploit Framework

Penetration testing is something that has already been discussed within this book, but it will be mentioned again. Within Kali Linux, you are granted access to all sorts of fantastic tools that can help you with your process of hacking, penetration testing, and searching for vulnerabilities or access points. One such tool for penetration testing that has not been discussed yet is a tool known as the Metasploit Framework. This particular tool utilizes Command line alterations or GUI. It can also be used as a sort of support method that can be used for all sorts of purposes. This tool is incredibly powerful and is used by both cybercriminals and ethical hackers alike due to the usefulness of the program.

In particular, Metasploit allows for the probing of any systematic vulnerabilities within a network or server, and is also open-source, meaning that the framework can be easily modified to work for anyone and with nearly any operating system.

What is Metasploit?

In particular, Metasploit refers to a specific tool that is used. The pen testing team that is using it will be able to use either code that was already made for them or custom code that they have created and then inject it into a network. In doing so, the flaws within that particular network become discovered and are brought to attention. This means then that they are able to address the weaknesses of that particular network so they can be addressed. Really, then, Metasploit is just another exploitative tool, much like Nmap, though it serves a different purpose. However, it is important to recognize that the tool itself is not evil or unethical. The tool itself is designed to be used for ethical hackers. The Metasploit Project came about in 2003 to use as a Perl-based portable network tool. However, by 2007, it was converted to Ruby and instead was licensed by Rapid7, where it has remained. Some of the tools within the Metasploit framework, which is larger than Metasploit itself, include several other tools that are regularly used within Kali Linux.

These tools all have different purposes and the Metasploit framework as becoming one of the default choices in development and mitigation. Before this, probes used to have to be performed manually, making pen testing incredibly slow-going, exhausting, and tedious. The framework has even grown to include some proprietary tools rather than the free offerings that have been built into Kali Linux. These tools, such as Metasploit Pro and Metasploit Express offer their own benefits, however, they are unnecessary if you do not want to use them.

Metasploit Users

Thanks to how wide the range of applications for Metasploit, it is used from ethical hackers that wish to make their own operating systems and servers more protected to those who are legitimately interested in breaking into an OS for nefarious purposes. It is, however, an incredibly reliable tool that is easy to install and useful.

No matter the language that you choose to use or which platform you are utilizing, Metasploit should work, and this is a pretty significant part of why Metasploit is so incredibly popular in the first place. It is so useful in making sure that it is readily accessible that it has become widespread. As of now, Metasploit includes over 1600 exploits for 25 different platforms, and it carries nearly 500 payloads. This all comes together to create such a powerful tool that people cannot help but enjoy it. Some of the payloads that are included are:

- **Command shell payloads:** They enable people to run scripts or commands against a different target or host

- **Dynamic payloads:** They allow testers to come up with unique payloads as they attempt to avoid any antivirus software

- **Meterpreter payloads:** They allow for the overtaking of device monitors to overtake other sessions

- **Static payloads:** They enable ports to be forwarded and communications to be had between networks.

Metasploit Modules

There are several modules included within Metasploit. These are core components—software that have very specific actions that they are supposed to perform. These also represent the actions that you can achieve within the Metasploit framework. These modules are readily located: all you have to do is find the following repository:

/path/to/metasploit/apps/pro/msf3/modules

The module type will be determined by the purpose of that particular one, as well as the action that the particular module is responsible for. In particular there are eight that are worthy of discussing.

These include:

- **Exploits:** Exploit modules are designed to execute a series of commands that then target a vulnerability that has been discovered within the targeted system or application. This module is designed to take advantage of any vulnerability in order to provide access to whatever the target system is. There are several different examples of exploit modules, such as code injection and web application exploits.

- **Payloads:** A payload refers to a shell code that runs after the exploit has managed to compromise the system at hand. The payload allows you to decide exactly how you want to be able to connect to the shell and what it is that you want to be done to the target after you have taken control of it. It can involve opening a meterpreter or a different command shell. The Meterpreter is specifically an advanced type of payload that allows for the writing of DLL files, allowing for new features as you need them to be created.

- **Encoders:** The encoders are critical tools that are able to convert one form of code into another.

- **Listeners:** Malware that is designed to hide to listen. When they are able to listen, they are able to gather up all sorts of important information, allowing for sensitive information, such as passwords, social security numbers, or other information that people would largely like to keep private to be leaked.

- **Auxiliary function:** Tools and commands meant to supplement the other functions of the device

- **Shellcode:** Code programmed to activate as soon as it is inside the target in order to do specific purposes, allowing for a more discrete way to get in and activate.

- **NOP generator:** This is a tool that is able to produce a series of random bytes that are designed to bypass any standard IDs in order to get past firewalls or important blockages.

- **Post-exploitation code:** The post-exploitation modules allow you to get more information or manage to steal further access within an exploited target. These include hash dumps or service enumerators.

Using Metasploit

When you have Metasploit installed and ready to use, all you need to do is gather information somehow, whether through first port scanning or finding a vulnerability scanner to find a way in.

Once you are in, all you have to do is choose an exploit and payload and Metasploit will do the rest for you. Effectively, the exploit is the way that weakness is identified and in harder to defend networks. The framework is specifically designed to make use of various models and interfaces, such as msfconsole interactive curses, and more. It can work from the terminal/cmd, and is also compatible with the Metasploit Community Web Interface, which will support pen testing.

Installing Metasploit

Before you can use Metasploit, however, you must first install it. Installing it will require you to first disable all of your firewalls and antivirus software. Due to the file itself, it is oftentimes considered malicious when you try to install it with your firewalls and antivirus software running. This then interrupts your installation. Because of this, it is best to just disable the firewall and antivirus software first before continuing. This means as well, however, that you must also make sure that you are ensuring that your source of download is legitimate and safe. If you are not careful, you may inadvertently download something that actually could be dangerous or problematic to you.

With the firewalls and antivirus software down, make sure that you also have your administrative privileges. This should not be a problem in Kali Linux as you should already have root user access by default, but if you are not for some reason or you are attempting to install Metasploit on a different distro of Linux, you are going to want to ensure that you also have that administrator privilege for yourself.

Finally, to install Metasploit, your best bet is to install it from the Rapid7 site. Doing so will allow you to get the installer for your specific operating system. It also will contain a self-contained environment that you can use for updating and running the framework. This means that everything that you need will all be taken care of during the initial installation process. You can, of course, go in manually to configure Metasploit yourself if you choose to do so, but that step is unnecessary and will be skipped for the purpose of this book. When you have the files, launch the installer. It will prompt you to enter a specific framework. As a Kali Linux user, you should find that this is preinstalled and not have to continue further.

Managing the Metasploit Database

Now, it is time to stop and finish the database information before continuing. When you are ready to manage your database, you will need to use the msfdb script to configure postgresql to run in order to store the database in ~/.msf4/db/

When ready to start this, you will use the following command:

$ msfdb init

This will trigger the database to start, and you will then be able to use any of several commands that will work best for you. These commands add extra functionality and help you manage the space that you have available. The most common commands at this stage that you will need to include:

msfdb reinit This will cause your database to be deleted and reinitialized in order to refresh it.

msfdb delete Using this particular command will lead to your database being deleted altogether without it reinitializing as the previous command caused.

msfdb start This command starts the database back up again, allowing it to begin running

msfdb stop This command, when used, will stop the database from running at all

msfdb status This command will allow the terminal to print the current database status, showing you all of the critical information within the terminal.

The Metasploit Datastore

Beyond just having everything that has been listed thus far, there is also the datastore—another core component of the Metasploit framework that is often overlooked altogether. This is a series of values that will allow you to configure any behaviors that you desire within the Metasploit framework. The datastore allows interfaces to change settings, while the payloads are able to patch up opcodes, and exploits are able to specify specific parameters. This also allows for the framework to pass between modules as well.

In particular, Metasploit has two different datastores: the global and module datastore. You will need to be familiar with both in order to use Metasploit effectively.

The global datastore can allow for all modules to use it. When the datastore option is set, all modules will have access to it. In order to define the global datastore option, you will need to use the command: setg

The module datastore, on the other hand, is designed so only designated modules will be able to utilize it, rather than anyone at all.

The Metasploit Workspaces

The workspaces within Metasploit allow you to segment up the hosts and data within the database. This allows you to use the workspaces to create separations between any of the segments that you wish to test. For example, imagine that you want a workspace for every single subnet within your organization because you want to limit the number of hosts to a specified network. This would lead to you creating workspaces such as one per department. This means that each organization's department would get its own workspaces.

When you use a workspace, you are able to import data, manipulate that data, and then export that data right back out in order to ensure that the data can be reused automatically. This also allows for the same workspace to automatically report anything about any current host that is being engaged with. This allows for information such as vulnerabilities to be transmitted.

If you wish to create a workspace, you must use the workspace command with the –a option in order to do so. Whatever workspace you create becomes the current one being used.

Imagine for a moment that you want one for the three departments, A, B, and C in your organization.

You would write:

msf workspace –a A

msf workspace –a B

ms workspace –a C

Overall, of course, if you are ready to use Metasploit, you should find that it is actually incredibly easy to get involved with. All you will need to know is how to go through the system and how to understand what you are looking at. When you know which kinds of modules are available, for example, you will be able to choose those that work for you. Because Metasploit is already jam-packed with all sorts of information for you that is designed to ensure that you are able to do almost anything with just a few commands instead of having to constantly manually be telling your system what you want it to do, it is actually incredibly user-friendly. This is exactly why it has become so popular.

Ultimately, you should be just fine with the free version that comes with Linux, though there are upgrades available if you care to pay for them, and ultimately, that will be a personal opinion and you will have to decide based on your own thoughts and desires. Of course, the upgraded versions, even though they boast quite the hefty price tags, are designed to be incredibly powerful for you. They are aimed at highly skilled pen tester professionals who know exactly what they are doing and exactly what they are getting, and they are able to justify that massive price tag. However, you do not have to do this as well.

Chapter 16: Digital Certificate

Just as how in the real world, we need to carry identification to prove who we are, especially when we are doing something major, such as buying a car or taking out a loan, your internet connection also needs some level of identification as well. This is where digital certificates come in. When you have servers full of valuable information, you likely want to ensure that your information is as protected as possible at all times—this makes sense. However, how are you supposed to be certain that those who are accessing the information on your server are truly who they said they were or truly allowed to be accessing it?

Especially in this day and age, when we are so concerned with data being stolen or taken over, it is easy to feel like our data is at risk, and for a good reason—it is. When you introduce a layer of digital certificates, however, you add an extra layer of safety to your servers or to feel like your private information is protected.

You are able to make sure that, though you are using sites that may be on the public internet, your data itself is certified.

If you have a LAN, however, you may not need this sort of major certification that would come along with using the public network for data. The cost of paying for those certificates may be unnecessary compared to the risk. In those instances, the best idea to secure a network is to use your own local CA or certificate authority—this will automatically sign any certificates that are actively installed within your LAN in order to protect their servers.

Most often, this is done with a tool known as OpenSSL—something that comes prepackaged with Kali Linux. We will be discussing how to create a certificate shortly, but for now, we will return our focus to the background information first.

This chapter will first discuss what a digital certificate and the certificate authorities that exist. From there, you will be walked through how to create a digital certificate on your Kali Linux based web servers. Being able to create your own digital certificate definitely has its own uses, but comes with its own issues as well. Nevertheless, if you think that it may be useful to you, you are more than welcome to pursue it. At the very least, it is more command language under your belt that you can use. At best, you may find some legitimate use in it.

What is a Digital Certificate?

The digital certificate is essentially the way to link the ownership of a public key on the internet to the individual that owns it. These are used for sharing public keys for encrypting and authenticating data. When you use these, you effectively end up with a way to safeguard the digital signature. Within a digital certificate, there are several layers of information that all serve different purposes—there is the public key that is certified. There is information that is identifying whoever is the owner of a said public key.
There is metadata that is directly related to the digital certificate, and there is a digital signature of that particular public key, generated by the certificate issuer.
Effectively, the public key comes in a pair—there is the public key that is used to lock the data that needs to be authenticated, and there is the private key that is held by the owner, used to sign and decrypt the protected data. Effectively, this leads to the digital certificate owner sharing the public key with their data that has been encrypted so they are able to access it with the private key that goes along with it.

These days most major web browsers utilize digital certificates—this allows people to know that the content that they are viewing has not been altered by someone who did not have permission to do so, and allows decrypting and encrypting of web content.

Effectively, this is just another way to develop the privacy and protection that people are looking for in their interactions with the internet. While you are able to issue your own PKI (public key infrastructure) and we will discuss doing that shortly, for the most part, there is some sort of organization that usually manages the creation and distribution of PKIs. This organization is known as the certificate authority.

Certificate Authorities

The certificate authority is a trusted third party who maintains the PKI, issuing out digital certificates and protecting them from being attacked or exploited in any way. By using a third party to authenticate a website and ensure that it is protected, websites are able to prove that they are actually safer than people may otherwise think. They are able to prove that they are legitimately interested and concerned in maintaining the safety of the customers and other people who are actively accessing their site because they are actively paying for that extra level of security.

The individuals feel like their data is better protected, which leads to a higher likelihood of people returning to that particular site again. They are willing to take the shot if they feel like they can trust the source.

Types of Certificates

Ultimately, there are several types of certificates that can be provided for an individual. These certificates either come from a different source or with a different purpose and they will be treated differently depending on the type of certificate that it is. The various certificates that can be used will be discussed in this section. The certificates exist in a sort of chain with each other, with one validating the other.

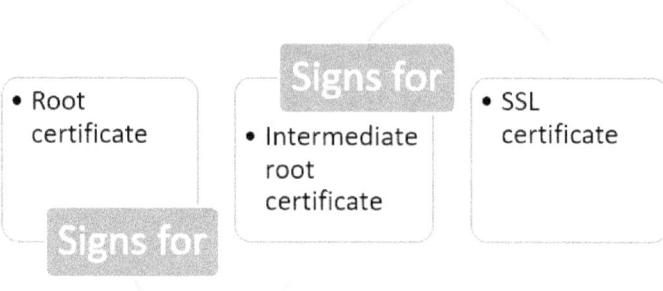

Root Certificate

The root certificate is a public key certificate that is meant to identify a root certificate authority (Root CA). Anyone is capable of generating a signing key and signing that new certificate, though it is not considered to be valid until it is signed by the trusted or valid CA. The root certificate is the top of the chain, essentially—it must be given by a trusted certificate. These are typically related to the software that you are using—if you are using Microsoft, for example, it is likely that your root certificate is signed by Microsoft.

Effectively, each of the certificate programs has its own sort of guidelines and stores of root certificates that can be used. These have the toughest standards for one reason—if you have one of these certificates, you are seen to be trusted. The root certificate is necessary in order to make sure that other certificates are issued and verified.

Intermediate Certificate

The intermediate certificate is the one in the middle—certificate authorities do not tend to directly issue their own certificates. Because of this, they instead use what is known as an intermediate root. This certificate is used by the CA to sign in and allow them to issue any end user SSL certificates. In doing this, there can be several intermediate root stops before you eventually arrive at the SSL certificate. Eventually, however, you reach the end user, who gets the SSL.

SSL Certificate

The final certificate, the end result, is the secure sockets layer—this is the global standard technology that allows for the use of encrypted communication between a browser and a server. These are used by millions of people and businesses everywhere to protect data from hackers or identity thieves. Effectively, the SSL allows for the conversation between the user and the server to be kept private, even though it is happening on the public web network.

These are typically issued by a certificate authority, who is trusted to ensure that the data will, in fact, be protected as promised. The SSL layer comes in several different types of certificates—they can be domain validated, organization validated, or extended validation.

Domain validated SSL certificates tell the least and promise the least—all you need to do to get this SSL is prove that you are using the right domain name. This does show that the data is being sent and received as intended to the one who holds the certificate, there is no way to prove who that certificate holder is.

Organization validated SSL certificates provide slightly more assurance—they confirm that the holder does have some sort of right or claim to use a specific domain but also undergo extra confirmation to ensure that the individual with the certificate does, in fact, own the domain. The extended validation certificate, on the other hand, is issued after applicants are able to prove that they are who they say they are to the standards of whatever CA is vetting them. This process requires the verification of the existence of the individual or entity who wishes to apply for the certificate, while also guaranteeing that the identity matches any official records as well. Effectively, the entity is verified and authorized to use that domain and certificate.

Generating Self-Signed SSL Certificates

As you are likely to expect, Kali Linux comes with its own program that allows it to create certificates. This is done through OpenSSL. While this will not always work for you and may, in fact, get rejected when you attempt to use it, you are able to do so.

You are able to provide all of the encryption benefits with your self-signed SSL certificate, but you will not get the authentication benefits. This means that not many people will be able to trust your site, and it is likely that anyone who tries to access your site will get a warning that says that your site or server is not, in fact, verified and therefore cannot be guaranteed.

Despite that, it can be useful to have, even if just for yourself. This section will discuss the steps necessary to create your own SSL certificates.

First, open up OpenSSL. There, you must use the following commands:

openssl genrsa –out key.pem 2048

openssl req –new –sha256 –key key.pem –out csr.csr

oepnssl req –x509 –sha256 –days 365 –key key.pem –in csr.csr –out certificate.pem

The first command triggers a 2048-bit RSA private key—this is the recommended format for your key to be in and it will be generated at that first command.

The second command triggers the creation of a certificate signing request—you will likely get questions at that second command and it is your job to answer them as accurately as possible to guarantee that you are seen as trustworthy. The third command triggers the generation of a self-signed x509 certificate that is usable on web servers. This is exactly what you were looking for. Remember, these will encrypt the site and make sure that your data is protected, but it does not actually offer authentication benefits. They can obviously still have their uses, such as when protecting a site during early stages, but due to the warning, you are not likely to want to keep this as your only form of verification if you will be expecting long-term traffic or you will be handling any sort of sensitive information such as payment methods or addresses.

Ultimately, you will need to figure out just how worthwhile paying for a legitimate certificate may be if you do not want to deal with security warnings chasing people away.

Chapter 17: Bash and Python Scripting

Bash itself is a shell—it stands for Bourne Again SHell, and it serves an important purpose. It allows for starting the server, confirming that the server is open, and working to keep everything running smoothly. Effectively, the shell on a system is meant to take any commands that you input through your keyboard in order to tell the operating system what to do. This was the only real way to interact with your Unix-like system back in the day, but these days, we have access to so much more. You are able to use GUIs alongside CLIs these days, meaning that you no longer have to type out what you want your computer to do if you want it to do so. This is why instead of typing out where your file is in order to locate it, you can simply go to your start menu, click, search through the files manually, and then open it up.

There is no denying that bash has a history—it is what was effectively initially used by those who were accessing their original systems, and while it was absolutely useful then, there is question now about whether it is still the best way to be interacting. It is like the stubborn old coworker that has been at her job forever and refuses to change, despite the fact that her way is clunky, inefficient, and really, redundant. Everyone would be happier if she went to the easier version, and productivity and ease of the work would go up, but she refuses.

This same sort of resistance appears with bash and transitioning from bash to another language, such as Python, which is currently one of the top contenders as a replacement. The idea these days is that the shell may be becoming obsolete—there are better ways to interact with your operating system. In particular, the shell has several concerning features:

- The syntax is obscure sometimes
- It is slow
- It is easy to accidentally leave out something crucial
- The shell's language's data structure is a string
- It is difficult to test units on the shell

Each of these lends their hands toward the idea of replacing the shell. While the shell has been used as a legitimate programming language, it is incomplete—it is not designed to be a complete programming language, but Python is.

Python itself is an interpreted, high-level programing language that is meant to be dynamic. It is meant to be object-oriented, it is meant to be layered. It is meant to be used as either a scripting language or even as a sort of binding agent between two different applications or components. Python is quite simple to learn and is focused on providing an easily readable system, allowing for it to be easier to access than some more complex languages that may emphasize old, outdated phrases or syntaxes that are simply used out of tradition and familiarity at this point. However, familiarity is not always a good thing.

Sometimes, what is needed more than ever is a change, or at least to adapt in some way in order to ensure that you are able to keep growing.

This is where Python and bash meet. Effectively, then, the best way to up productivity would be from moving away from the use of the shell and instead, work with Python code instead. Because Python is easier to read, is faster, and allows for legitimate testing, it seems like shifting over to it, at least in some capacity would be beneficial.

Interestingly enough, Python is already installed by default on major Linux distributions. If you were to open a command prompt and type in "**python**" you should be provided with a Python interpreter. This alone suggests that it may be worth the use of Python over bash when considering the creation of scripting. Thanks to the ease of use alone, it would save time.

Take a look at some of the most compelling reasons to shift from focusing on shell scripts to using Python as a replacement instead:

- **It is installed by default**
- **It is easy to read and the syntax is simple**
- **It is an interpreted language**

- It is a fully-featured programming language

- Python has access to a standard library and plenty of third-party libraries in order to use all sorts of utilities

- Python's standard library is sorted by date and time, allowing you to put a date into any format to compare it to other dates

- Python is a simpler transitional link

The assertion here is not to step away from the shell altogether—the shell absolutely has its own purposes. However, the shell also is weak in several aspects. Think about how much nicer it would be to navigate through several of your tasks in a much simpler manner—it would be nice to have syntax and commands that make more sense rather than being remembered simply because of you now that you were supposed to remember them.

Of course, there are areas where bash is, undoubtedly simpler. This is exactly why the two should be brought together.

When they are drawn together, they are able to bring out the best in each other—you will have the best of both worlds thanks to having a system that is capable of transitioning between the two with ease. Python is more complete and more readily used in several different contexts whereas bash was designed with Linux in mind. It is impossible to deny that some of bash is just nicer to use. For example, consider moving a file from your desktop to a directory on bash:

cd Desktop# mv folder directory

Notice how nice and neat that is.

Now, in Python, it would look more like:

Import os globfor fname in glob.glob ('folder'):os.rename (fname, 'directory')

There is no denying that the Python code is unnecessarily bulky, especially when standing next to that short and sweet blurb from bash.

This is exactly why it would be best to utilize the two together rather than trying to disentangle them and replacing one or the other.

While we have already discussed that it is possible for you to bring in your Python code within your shell, it is also possible to go the other direction as well—you can introduce your Python script within your shell and you can insert your shell scripts within Python as well. All you need to do is import the OS module. If you do so, you will be able to make use of your bash commands within Python as well—this means that you are effectively able to mix and match your commands with ease. Think of how children who have grown up speaking two languages at home tend to seamlessly shift from one to the next within the same sentence, inserting a few words in one language while also inserting some of the other languages interchangeably, creating what sounds like something that would be impossible to understand, but they do so with ease. This is what you would be doing with Python by inserting bash as well.

In order to bring bash language to python, all you have to do is:

$ python >>>from os import *>>> system ('sudo apt-get update')

And you should now have access to both languages.

You should absolutely try to tinker around with both languages. If you are not familiar with Python yet, you may feel inclined to go through the effort of learning it—it is incredibly simple to pick up and if you were already able to pick up communicating with Linux, you should be able to pick up understanding Python as well. All you have to do is put in some of the efforts that once went to developing your skills with Linux toward learning this system as well. You will likely find that with the increased productivity, you will quickly grow fond of the change.

If you are unsure whether you have Python currently installed on your system, you are in luck—finding out, you will need to enter the following command:

$ python –version

You will most likely get an older and stable form of Python that is sufficient, but you will likely want to upgrade that form into the more recent version. This version is constantly changing, so it is for the best if you go check the version that is available to you upon reading this book—you can do this by simply searching for the most recent version online and then updating.

If you do decide to pursue Python in particular, you will want to go and find some guides and books, not unlike this one that you are reading right now to find out what you need to know. Tutorials and web lessons are always fantastic starting stones for you to begin experimenting with Python. Eventually, as you become more comfortable and familiar, you may decide to begin intertwining your attempts to use both languages together. You may even decide that you prefer Python over using the shell, and that is fine too.

If you want to learn or improve your knowledge about Python programming language, I recommend my book

Python: 2 Books in 1 - Python Programming + Python Machine Learning

With this book you will learn quickly and effectively the most used programming language.

Ultimately, technology is changing so rapidly that you cannot afford to hold yourself back with a fear of changing or growing or shifting to something new—transitioning and learning are absolutely beneficial to you.

Now, as this chapter and this book come to a close, it is time for you to begin thinking about how to put everything together. It is time to consider whether you are really interested in Kali Linux at all or if you would prefer to learn something else. What is for sure, however, is that ultimately, you must guide yourself and your own decisions in order to ensure that you are happy with what you have chosen to do.

Conclusion

Congratulations—you have made it to the end of *Kali Linux Hacking*. This book is designed to be a crash course in learning Kali Linux—the operating system designed specifically for penetration testing by penetration testing professionals for the use of finding and repairing any sorts of weaknesses or exploits that are found within the system. If you have made it this far, you must have been quite interested in either installing Kali Linux, or you have used this book as a guide, and regardless of which of those holds true, thank you for joining me on this journey.

Within this book, you were provided with basic information for Kali Linux. As a reminder once more, Kali Linux is not a beginner's distro for Linux. If you have read this book and are entirely lost on several subjects, that is okay—but you may be better off starting with a beginner's book instead of one designed for people who know what they are doing and are interested in doing better and more.

Ultimately, your next step is entirely dependent upon you and what you think you want to do. Do you want to practice on the actual distribution of Kali Linux? You may go through the information and effort necessary to install your own copy that you can begin to use and discover. If you feel like Kali Linux is not right for you, whether due to it being too difficult, too different, or simply because you do not know what you are doing, then you are probably better off with starting with something simpler, such as Ubuntu and Mint.

Yes, this point has been reiterated several times because it is that important. Even after having read through this guide, if you are not entirely confident in yourself and your abilities, it may be better for you to forego Kali Linux temporarily while you build up your skills—and that is okay.

Perhaps at this point, you have taken the advice of the final chapter in this book and have decided to look into Python as well, bettering your scripting abilities so you will be able to better utilize your own commands. That is also a fantastic decision to make and will help guide you on your journey as well, simply because you will have that much more knowledge.

No matter what you choose to do next, whether it is pursuing more knowledge about Linux in general or attempting to figure out how best to interact with Kali Linux that you have already installed, one thing is for sure: You have hopefully learned something during the process of reading this book. It is with the utmost hope as this book wraps to a close that you have found this book informative, helpful, and insightful to the grand world of Kali Linux and everything it has to offer. No matter whether you are a newbie or someone with familiarity with other Linux distros, good luck on your endeavors, and remember—just because you feel like things may be complicated now does not mean that you have to give up on it. You can put in the effort to learn if you want to, and with that effort will come results. Good luck and remember to keep your penetration testing ethical.

And finally, if you have found this book to be informative, insightful, enjoyable, actionable, or otherwise beneficial to you, please do not hesitate to leave a review with your insight and feedback on Amazon. Your feedback and opinion is always greatly appreciated. Thank you once more for accompanying me on this journey, and good luck.

www.ingramcontent.com/pod-product-compliance
Lightning Source LLC
Chambersburg PA
CBHW071355210526
45465CB00001B/94